Haydn

H. C. R.

H.C. ROBBINS LANDON

HAYDN
Symphonies

BBC MUSIC GUIDES

ARIEL MUSIC
BBC PUBLICATIONS

Published by BBC Publications
A division of BBC Enterprises Ltd
35 Marylebone High Street, London WIM 4AA

ISBN 0 563 20515 6

First published 1966
Reprinted 1968, 1972, 1975, 1976, 1982
First published in Ariel Music 1986

Typeset in 10/11 pt Garamond by Phoenix Photosetting, Chatham
Printed in England by Mackays of Chatham Ltd

Contents

Haydn's Precursors

THE SYMPHONIES FOR COUNT MORZIN AT LUKAVEC
(1757 OR 1758 TO MAY 1761)

It was often asserted, in the nineteenth century, that Haydn invented
the symphony and the string quartet. Recent research has shown that he
did actually invent the string quartet as we know it, but that the symphony was a flourishing form long before Haydn began to compose.
Johann Stamitz, the greatest of the famous Mannheim school, wrote
several dozen symphonies before his death in 1757; and 1757 is the very
earliest date for Haydn's first symphonies. Haydn lived in Vienna after
his expulsion from St Stephen's Cathedral in 1749 – his voice had
broken and the *Kapellmeister*, Georg Reutter, used the first pretext he
could find to dismiss the young Haydn – and in the ensuing decade the
composer studied and eked out a living by playing violin and organ, and
by teaching. In 1757 – the date has been securely established through
the research of the Austrian scholar, Fritz Dworschak[1] – he composed
his first string quartets in the summer castle, Weinzierl (near Melk in
Lower Austria), of K. J. W. von Fürnberg; it was Fürnberg who recom-
mended Haydn to another Austrian nobleman, Count Morzin, who
engaged the composer supposedly in 1759. Morzin's summer castle was
at Lukavec in Bohemia, and Haydn told his biographers Griesinger and
Dies that he wrote his first symphony (No. 1) in 1759 for Morzin;
Griesinger even quotes the *incipit*. Haydn's memory, when he recalled
all these events of his youth, was no longer wholly reliable; the basic
facts are, of course, true, but the dates are not always correct. For some
years, scholars have rather doubted that Haydn's first symphony was
composed in 1759. For one thing, Breitkopf & Härtel, the famous
Leipzig publishing house, sent the composer a list of works attributed to
him, asking him to discard those that were spurious. Haydn divided the
list in ten groups, from 1757 to 1797 (actually his last symphony was
composed in 1795), so that 1757 seemed to have stuck in his mind as
the year in which he began to compose symphonies. Recently, new evidence has come to light which supports 1757 rather than 1759: a manuscript in the Bohemian castle of Český Krumlov (German: Krummau),
the seat of the Schwarzenberg family, has come to light – a copy of
Haydn's Symphony No. 37 with the date 1758 on the cover. Thus we
now have written evidence that Haydn was composing symphonies by

1 'Joseph Haydn und Karl Joseph Weber von Fürnberg', in *Unsere Heimat, Monatsblatt
des Vereines für Landeskunde und Heimatschutz von Niederösterreich und Wien*, 1932.

1758. Does this negate the composer's assertion that Symphony No. 1 actually was his first work in the form? I think not necessarily: it is entirely possible that Haydn's memory was correct and that No. 1 *was* No. 1, but that it was composed in 1757 or 1758, and not in 1759.

Haydn had written numerous works before he wrote his first symphony. The reason that he composed no symphony before he was engaged by Morzin is probably a very simple one: no one asked him to. In the eighteenth century, composers generally wrote for a specific occasion in mind, and the idea of a composer writing a symphony for the desk drawer, as Schubert did, was inconceivable fifty or a hundred years earlier. In a sense, the whole of the Vienna classical school is one glorious series of *Gelegenheitsmusik* or, if you will, *Gebrauchsmusik*: in the strict use of the word, Mozart's *Figaro*, Handel's *Israel in Egypt* and Haydn's symphonies are all *pièces d'occasion*.

Although, as we have noted, Haydn wrote no symphonies before *c.* 1757 he did write clavichord sonatas, keyboard concertos, church music, string quartets, string trios (two violins and *basso*, or rather violoncello), and an opera (*Der neue krumme Teufel*), so that by 1757 he was a skilled craftsman. He had also written a number of divertimenti for strings and wind instruments which reveal his innate sense of compact form and his passionate addiction to working with, and developing his musical structure from, small motives. These pre-symphony compositions also reveal a born gift for orchestration and a particular flair for the wind instruments, especially the French horn (*corno da caccia*, or hunting horn), an instrument that Haydn treated affectionately his life long. In these years, he also had an opportunity of studying symphonies by his contemporaries. Scholars have often tried to find the origins of Haydn's symphonic form, and usually they have been singularly unsuccessful. The Mannheim school, which German scholars, some half a century ago, put forward as Haydn's precursors, is now known to have been much more isolated in its influence than was previously asserted; and it is interesting to see how very few of the typical mannerisms of the Mannheim school (long series of *crescendi* and *diminuendi*, and a marked avoidance of the strong recapitulation) can be found in Haydn's music. The Austrians, annoyed at the German claim to have found Haydn's true musical origins, then put forward G. M. Monn (1717–50), who composed a four-movement symphony with a minuet in 1740 (autograph in the Vienna National Library), as Haydn's principal precursor. But Monn was not an important composer and his much-vaunted four-movement symphony was, historically, a flash-in-the-pan; most Austrian symphonies of the 1750s have three, not four, movements.

Examination of the Austrian archives would long ago have revealed Haydn's immediate precursors. The great Benedictine monasteries of Göttweig and Lambach and Kremsmünster – to name but three – have dated copies of symphonies and in the case of the first two houses highly important thematic catalogues (doubly important because some of the dated copies they list no longer exist). The percentage of Mannheim symphonies is very small indeed – almost worth discarding entirely so far as Haydn's musical origins are concerned. The Austrians themselves had several highly talented composers who wrote symphonies in the 1750s, of which possibly the most important were Florian Leopold Gassmann (1729–74), Georg Christoph Wagenseil (1715–77) and Carlos d'Ordoñez (1734?–86), while among the most interesting symphonies were the first products of Leopold Hofmann (1738–93), which reached Leipzig as early as 1760. The American musicologist, Jan La-Rue, has demonstrated that 'it was he [Hofmann] and not Haydn who established securely the four-movement form, including slow introduction and minuet, of the concert symphony',[1] as opposed to the three-movement operatic overture (Italian: *sinfonia*) in which most of Haydn's early symphonies, as well as those of his contemporaries, are cast.

The 'Mannheim *crescendo*' with which Haydn's Symphony No. 1 begins has often been cited as proof that he must have studied the music of, say, Johann Stamitz. But again, we have evidence that Haydn learned of this new orchestral device nearer at home; for the three-movement overture (*sinfonia*) to Gassmann's opera, *L'issipile*,[2] composed in 1758 for Venice, opens in the same fashion, and the other two movements are similar in style and orchestral texture to Haydn's work:

EX. 1

(a) Gassman: L'issipile[3]

1 *Die Musik in Geschichte und Gegenwart*, article 'Symphonie', Vol. XII, col. 1812.
2 Edited by the author in the series, *Diletto musicale*, Verlag Doblinger (Vienna–Munich, 1965).
3 Gassmann, *L'issipile* overture (1758).

EX. 1 (continued)

(b) Haydn: Symphony No. 1[1]

Haydn's Austrian contemporaries experimented not only with the inner style of their music – such as the Mannheim excursion quoted above – but also with the outward scheme. Having been born as a three-movement operatic overture (fast-slow-fast, the two latter movements generally in quicker time, 2/4, 3/8, 6/8, than the opening movement, which is usually in four-four or barred *alla breve*, sometimes in 3/4), they began to introduce the minuet, usually in third place, and sometimes a slow introduction. But in a symphony by Carlos d'Ordoñez, of which Göttweig Abbey owns a copy dated 1756, there is a whole opening slow movement and then an *allegro*: this scheme derives from the old Italian *sonata da chiesa*, and it was a device that Haydn later adopted in several of his symphonies (Nos. 11, 18, 21, 22, 34, 49). It is also a characteristic of Austrian concert symphonies that the themes of the quick movements are often of more rhythmic than melodic importance:

EX. 2

(a)[2]

---

1 Haydn, Symphony No. 1 (supposedly 1759; perhaps 1758?).
2 d'Ordoñez *Sinfonia* in C (Modena, Bib. Estense E 172).

It was primarily J. B. Vanhal (1739–1813) – he spent many years in Italy – who brought the singing *allegro* to the Austrian symphony:

EX. 3[3]

This marriage between Italian operatic melody and Austrian work-manship was later to determine Mozart's style (*e.g.* the first *allegro* of the E flat Symphony, K543).

In the late 1750s, however, Haydn's principal subjects are con-structed not so much as intrinsically beautiful, singable themes but in small motivic segments with strong rhythmic elements which can be isolated and used to develop the material. The modulation to the domin-ant does not usually mean that Haydn introduces a contrasting second subject; rather he prefers to introduce part or the whole of the first subject in the dominant, whereas his second subjects have rather the character of codettas. The first movement of Symphony No. 17 is typical in this respect, and you will find it in the first movement of Haydn's very last symphony, No. 104.

In fact, only a thorough understanding of the principles of sonata form will make Haydn's music fully intelligible; in this respect he is far more intellectual than Mozart, who is always at pains to see that his music sounds beautiful, that the melodies are in the singing tradition, and that the inner parts are also intrinsically interesting. Haydn, even in his earliest symphonies, will write whole passages in two-part harmony (violins together, viola doubling the bass line) with subjects which are not 'singable' at all: whereas Mozart's tunes almost always fit the human

1 d'Ordoñez *Sinfonia* in A (Göttweig Abbey dated 1764; Osek Abbey, now Prague National Library 344A; Doksy Castle, now Prague; Pachta Coll., Prague XXII E-13; Brussels Conservatoire 7779).
2 d'Ordoñez *Sinfonia* in D (Thurn und Taxis Archives, Regensburg; Osek Abbey 345A).
3 J. B. Vanhal, *Sinfonia* in B flat (announced in the Breitkopf Catalogue of 1774).

voice, Haydn's usually grow out of the orchestra; thus the first movement of Mozart's *Haffner* Symphony, with its octave jumps and strong rhythmic-motivic nature, is something of an exception, as is the beautiful *cantabile* theme that opens Haydn's Symphony No. 21:

EX. 4

Haydn's orchestration is also entirely different from Mozart's. Haydn's use of C major, with *alto* (high) horns, trumpets, and timpani (Symphonies 20, 32, 33, 38, 41, 48, 50, 56, 82, 90), involves him in a very characteristic orchestral sound which is high-pitched (also literally in the horns) and highly strung – it sounds nothing like Mozart at all. There is also, in most of the opening movements in Haydn's earlier symphonies, a nervous drive which occasionally, as in Symphony No. 24/1,[1] rises to almost unbearable heights of tension.

The chronological list of 104 Haydn symphonies is now known to be rather faulty: since it was prepared for the now defunct Breitkopf & Härtel Complete Edition nearly sixty years ago, many new and dated sources have come to light and, moreover, the old list was deliberately laid out to give each undated work its latest possible date. The worst mistake is No. 72, which ought to be about forty or fifty numbers earlier. Three indubitably genuine symphonies were omitted: the so-called Symphonies 'A' and 'B' and a lost work in D major which Haydn entered in his own Draft Catalogue (*Entwurf-Katalog*). Recently a whole collection of Morzin-period symphonies has come to light in Hungary; they were owned by a Lieutenant-Colonel Fürnberg who was presumably a relative of Haydn's friend von Fürnberg, for whom he created the string quartet. Haydn made some corrections in the parts of this collection, which is thus most important: not a single autograph of the Morzin symphonies has survived, so that textually these Hungarian copies are of

1 This abbreviation will be used throughout; it means the first movement of Symphony No. 24. No. 24/III means the third movement.

the utmost value. So far as we can determine, the following symphonies were composed between 1757 or 1758 and 1761 (in May of the latter year Haydn was engaged by Prince Esterházy, as we shall see): Nos. 'A', 1–5, 10, 11, 15, 18, 27, 32, 33, and 37 – this is the list of works in the newly discovered Fürnberg Collection. To these should probably be added Nos. 'B', 19, and 20, though it is difficult to understand why they should have been omitted from the Fürnberg series of manuscripts: perhaps they were once included and have since disappeared. In any case none of the three can have been composed much later than 1761. No. 25 has a slow introduction but no slow movement; stylistically it might have been written at any time between c. 1760 and c. 1764.

The formal scheme of these earliest Haydn symphonies is very varied. Some are in the usual Italian operatic *sinfonia* form with three movements (*e.g.* Nos. 'A' and 1); No. 4 has as its third movement a 'Tempo di Minuet'. Some have four movements, but often the minuet comes second (Nos. 15, 'B', 32, 33, 37). Three have entire opening slow movements in the church-sonata tradition (Nos. 5, 11, and 18), but No. 18, instead of having four movements, has only three, closing with a 'Tempo di Menuet'. No. 15 has a very interesting opening movement in the old French *ouverture* form of slow-fast-slow, something Haydn never did again in a symphony. Apart from these widely varying outward differences, the formal designs within the various symphonies are highly flexible. In No. 2, for instance, Haydn abolishes all the repeat signs (usually each movement is divided in two, with repeat signs in the middle and at the end). The finale of No. 3 is a fugue, or rather a double fugue, in the manner of J. J. Fux, the famous Austrian contrapuntist and composer whose textbook, *Gradus ad Parnassum*, Haydn admired and always gave his students to use. In the opening movement of No. 5, Haydn borrows a leaf from the divertimento and gives whole sets of solo passages to the horns: here and in the trio, which is also divertimento-like, Haydn writes up to a" (actual sound) for the first horn, making this symphony one of the most difficult for the horn in the entire literature. As for the scoring of these works, the basic orchestration is oboes, horns, and strings, to which a bassoon and harpsichord were added to the *basso continuo* as a matter of course. In Symphony 'B', a bassoon suddenly makes a solo appearance in the trio; this also happens in Symphony No. 9 of 1762; the rest of the time it played with the bass line and was probably silent in *pianissimo* passages and perhaps during the slow movements. Usually the wind instruments are dropped in the slow movements – but not, characteristically, in the church-sonata works. In

Nos. 20, 32, and 33 trumpets and kettledrums are added. It is not until 1774 that Haydn uses trumpets and timpani in a key other than C major (the timpani part in No. 13 is added to the autograph manuscript in an unknown hand and that to No. 72, composed about the same time as No. 13, *i.e.* 1763, exists only in one manuscript and is dubious) and then only sparingly (No. 54 in G, afterwards in a few works in D).

There is one outstanding quality that always characterizes these early symphonies: the innate, impeccable craftsmanship and the astoundingly sure sense of form (in itself the mark of a craftsman). On the whole, these works do not plumb the emotional heights and depths of Haydn's later music, but there is a sense of object, of economical means (Haydn's music is *never* garrulous), that must have made his contemporaries sit up and take notice. All these works were widely circulated throughout the Habsburg dominions in manuscript parts, for printing of music did not really take hold in Austria until the 1780s; pirated copies were soon sent to France – the centre of European music in those days – and published. Haydn obviously made some money from marketing manuscript copies – the Fürnberg Collection shows that he 'supervised' the work – but he never saw a penny from the enormous sales of his music in Paris, and it is probable that he never even saw copies of many of those pirated French editions. If we may sum up the quality of Haydn's early symphonies by comparing them with those of his contemporaries, it is clear that most of Haydn's symphonic works are the equal of those by d'Ordoñez, Wagenseil, Hofmann, Gassmann or Michael Haydn, Joseph's younger brother, who was writing symphonies in Grosswardein (Oradea Mare, now Rumania) by 1760: one of his autographs is signed '*Partita* [another word for symphony in those days] 5ta . . . 20ma 9bris [November] 760 [1760]'. But some of Haydn's early symphonies go further than that: the ghostly syncopations of No. 4/II; the thundering pomp of the opening movements of Nos. 20, 32, and 33; the glittering brilliance of the middle section of No. 15/I, flanked by a magical slow section with real touches of poetry; the stately dignity of No. 4's 'Tempo di Minuet' with its beautiful *pp* (exaggerated dynamic marks in Haydn are always used to point up some structural tautening, some felicitous detail: they are, in a word, always meaningful) – all these things placed Haydn, then in his late twenties, as a composer of immense talent who was even then beginning to tower over his contemporaries. Nevertheless, if these early symphonies were all that were known of Haydn, his name would be no more illustrious today than those of d'Ordoñez or Hofmann or Michael Haydn.

The Symphonies for Eisenstadt (1761–5)

THE FIRST ESTERHÁZY PERIOD

Count Morzin seems to have run into financial difficulty and was forced to abandon his band. It appears that Prince Paul Anton Esterházy heard Haydn conduct a concert at Morzin's when the band was still in existence, and at any rate, Esterházy engaged Haydn as his *Vice Kapellmeister* in May 1761. The old Gregor Werner was nominal head of music for Esterházy, but Haydn was placed in charge of the orchestra. At the time of Haydn's engagement, the band was greatly enlarged: it consisted of two flutes (whose players could also perform on other instruments), two oboes, one bassoon (another could be had if necessary), four horns (at the beginning only two), and strings. Trumpets and timpani could be taken from the 'tower music' of Eisenstadt, and there was always someone available to play the timpani when the old timpanist Adam Sturm was pensioned off in 1771. It is a little difficult for us to reconstruct the exact size of Haydn's string group in 1761, but the scores of the first symphonies he wrote for Eisenstadt show that he must have had available at least six violins, two or three violas, three cellists, and two double-bass players (who used the *violone* with its lowest string C, sounding three octaves below middle C, not E as it is today). Later, in the 1780s, Haydn's orchestra consisted of twenty-four players of which the following were the wind players: a flute, two oboes, two bassoons, and two horns. The trumpets and timpani were not included in the list and had to be recruited for special occasions. Haydn conducted operas from the harpsichord and concerts with the violin-bow.

While we have not been able to find any documents concerning Morzin's band, Haydn's activities at Eisenstadt and, later, Eszterháza (Esterház) are well documented; Hungarian as well as Austrian scholars are now engaged in publishing the day-to-day receipts from instrument makers, lists of salaries, and so forth, which provide many interesting details about Haydn and the instrumental and vocal performers at the court. In the early 1760s the band was usually located at Eisenstadt, but they occasionally went to Kittsee Castle, a pretty residence across the Danube from what was then Pressburg (now Bratislava, Czechoslovakia). In a document of the year 1765 we read that Haydn is 'to hold in our {Prince Esterházy's} absence two musical concerts every week in the Officers' room at Eisenstadt, *viz.* on Tuesdays and Saturdays from two to four o'clock in the afternoon. All the musicians shall appear . . .'. There is no doubt that most of Haydn's new symphonies were first performed at these bi-weekly concerts at Eisenstadt.

The first works that Haydn composed for Prince Esterházy were three programmatic symphonies entitled *Le Matin, Le Midi*, and *Le Soir* (Nos. 6–8) which are scored for one or (in No. 7) two flutes, oboes, a bassoon, two horns, and strings; the strings include one or two solo violins – Haydn divides them in the old concerto grosso tradition of *concertino* and *ripieno* – a solo cello and a solo double bass (*violone*). These three works are an astonishing combination of concerto grosso, divertimento, concerto, suite, and symphony. In part Haydn chose to return to the instrumental lay-out, and the then antiquated language, of the baroque concerto grosso; altogether there are many sections of these symphonies (*e.g.* the trio of No. 6) which sound far more baroque than anything in the symphonies composed for Morzin. In the succeeding years, Haydn was to turn with increasing frequency to baroque forms, and to counterpoint, for inspiration. In No. 3 he had written a double fugue for the finale: he repeated this in No. 40 (a misplaced work, chronologically – it was composed in 1763 and belongs next to No. 13) and in the famous fugal finales of the String Quartets, Op. 20 (1772). Another typical feature of these Eisenstadt symphonies is the use of solo instruments in the manner of the concerto: we find it in all three of the programmatic symphonies, but these are special works. The second movement of Symphony No. 13 could be the slow movement of a cello concerto, the slow movement of No. 24 from a flute concerto. In No. 36 (another misplaced work) the slow movement returns to the concerto grosso traditions of Nos. 6–8. On the whole, most of the new symphonies had a minuet (Nos. 12, 16 and 17 are exceptions), usually in third place. (Curiously: the Quartets of Op. 17, 1771, have them in second place, and so does Symphony No. 44, probably composed in that year.)

In 1762, Prince Paul Anton died and was succeeded by Prince Nicolaus, under whom Haydn served till the prince's death in 1790. For the first three years, Haydn's outward life changed little; but as we shall see, 1766 saw a far-reaching change in Haydn's circumstances, and it is thus convenient, and stylistically valid, to consider the years 1761–5 as an entity. It is perhaps useful to provide a survey of the symphonies composed in these years; whereas no autographs of the Morzin symphonies have survived, of the early Esterházy years a goodly number still exists, so that the chronological problems are slightly reduced. Here are the dated works:

1761: Nos. 6, 7, 8 (*Le Matin, Le Midi, Le Soir*)
1762: No. 9
1763: Nos. 12, 13, 40
1764: Nos. 21, 22, 23, 24
1765: Nos. 28, 29, 30, 31

The undated works that fall in this period are Nos. 14 (*c.* 1761–3), 16 (*c.* 1760–3), 17 (*c.* 1760–2), 36 (*c.* 1761–5), and 72 (*c.* 1763–5). Adding these to those with known dates we have a total of twenty symphonies spread over five years, or an average of four each year. The undated ones (except No. 72, which cannot have been composed earlier than 1763, the year when Haydn's band was enlarged from two to four horn players) probably fill in 1761 and 1762, for it is very unlikely that Haydn wrote only one symphony in the latter year.

Symphony No. 9 has no finale at all. In 1762, several Haydn operas were performed at Eisenstadt, and possibly this symphony served as the overture to one of them. For his opera *Acide e Galatea* (1762) Haydn wrote a three-movement overture which was circulated in manuscript as a symphony; indeed, there is very little difference between it and one of Haydn's early, three-movement concert symphonies. It was the last time that Haydn made no difference between overture and symphony; from this point, the two forms go separate, though related, ways.

In 1763, as we have noted, the band was increased to include four horn players. Probably to show Prince Nicolaus how elegant four horns sounded, Haydn composed Symphony No. 13, which boasts a flute, two oboes, four horns, and timpani (added later to the autograph by an unknown hand but patently under Haydn's supervision, because the part was circulated later by professional copyists and turns up again at Harburg Castle in Bavaria – though the manuscript is Viennese in origin – and also in Bohemia). Haydn uses this relatively large wind band like an organ: it holds massive chords through which the strings dart in tight rhythmic figures. It is interesting to see that Haydn 'spaces' his horn chords in the modern way, *i.e.* I–III and II–IV; Haydn was always very forward-looking in the matter of technical notation for his musicians, and he was writing timpani in real (as opposed to transposed) notation while Mozart was still writing C-G for tonic-dominant whatever the key. We shall return to this matter again in considering the London symphonies.

Haydn was now at great pains to provide his listeners at Eisenstadt with a constant variety of symphonies. Apart from writing movements which might be from a concerto, he turns to all manner of devices to make each work different from the last. In 1764 he wrote two symphonies in the church-sonata form with opening slow movements (Nos. 21, 22): both are particularly fine works, but No. 22, which is known as 'The Philosopher' (for no reason we can now determine), is one of the most striking of these early symphonies. It is scored for two cors anglais, horns, and strings, and the opening movement is a kind of chorale-prelude, wherein the wind instruments intone the theme very loudly against a constant procession of marching quavers in the strings. In many respects the first movement of No. 24 is one of the highpoints of Haydn's nervous style: to drive the music forward he had, in the development section, marked *ff* at the beginning of each bar; and the pace is so tense that he is forced to bring in the recapitulation *piano* (it was at the beginning *forte*) and in the tonic minor, after a pause to allow the exhausted listeners – and players – to catch their breath. The use of accents, which Haydn marks *fz* or *forz* (=*forzato*: literally, 'forced') as opposed to Mozart's *sf* (*sforzato*), gradually begins to assume an ever greater meaning in Haydn's music. Usually these accents are placed off the beat and add to the already natural tension of a syncopated passage: it was one of the most important details of Haydn's style and Beethoven later took it over intact. Haydn's music is often very nervous and these accents make an unsettled and hard-driven line even more dramatic. Haydn also prefers abrupt dynamic contrasts to smoother *crescendi* and *decrescendi*, marks that he rarely uses until the 1770s, and then for the most part in slow movements, where the stately pace was, he felt, more suited to gradual dynamic gradations. But in the 1760s, there are whole movements where there are only two dynamic levels – loud and soft. Such a movement, perhaps carried to its furthest point, is the opening of No. 24. In his finales, too, Haydn constantly sought to get away from the rather trite 2/4 or 3/8 of his own early symphonies and those of his precursors. The finale of No. 23 is a witty *perpetuum mobile* which actually stutters at the end and leaves us with a single hushed pizzicato chord.

The four known symphonies of the year 1765 are also immensely varied. No. 28 in A opens with a movement which sounds like 6/8 for the first few bars but is actually in 3/4; the whole movement is based on and dominated by the rhythmic pulse of the opening ♩ ♫♫ | ♩. The 'Menuet' goes at the fastest tempo Haydn has yet marked for such a dance form – *allegro molto*; it has some bizarre effects whereby the same note is repeated with open and fingered strings. The trio sounds like a forlorn gipsy dance: Haydn was obviously fascinated by the folk-lore of the Balkans, and as an exotic effect often introduced Balkan melodies or what one might call 'mood music' from the East. (There is a most striking example of the latter in the trio of the next symphony, No. 29 in E.) As opposed to the almost total lack of a melody in the opening movement of No. 28, the *allegro di molto* (Haydn took quite a time making up his mind what the tempo should be – his first thought was *allegro ma non troppo*) of No. 29 has a singing, almost Italian melody for its first subject. To contrast this with the finale, in the latter Haydn writes one of his *furioso* movements in which there is only one brief section in *piano*: everything else tears along *forte* with urgent crotchets pounding away in the bass.

The first movement of Symphony No. 30 in C (*Alleluja*) uses the old Gregorian Easter Alleluia melody, with the first note changed from A to G. (It exists in this corrupted version also in eighteenth-century plainsong books):

EX. 5

Perhaps the most sensational of all these early Eisenstadt symphonies are No. 31 in D, known in Austria and Germany as 'mit dem Hornsignal', and No. 72 in D: they are both elaborate 'hunting' symphonies which feature not only four virtuoso horn parts but also difficult *soli* for the other wind instruments and *concertante* violin, cello, and even double-bass (*violone*) parts. Both end with suite-like variation movements in which each variation, after the theme has been announced, is allotted to one or more solo instruments. In the second movements of each, the concerto-grosso method of *concertino* (the 'solo' group) and *ripieno* (the main body), which we noted in Nos. 6–8 and also the slow movement of No. 36, obtains. In the *adagio* of No. 31 the *concertino* group consists of the four horns, two in G and two in D, with solo violin and solo cello; in the *andante* of No. 72, the *concertino* is the flute and a solo violin. Although the finales are in slow tempo, they both end with a *presto* which is a kind of *Kehraus* (the 'go-home' signal for an evening of dance music); but in No. 31 the whole work is structurally, and musically, unified by the fact that the rousing horn calls of the beginning also serve to close the symphony. In some respects No. 72 – fine though it is – sounds like a study for the more perfect and perhaps more sophisticated No. 31. In a way, this generous, warm-hearted music seems like a farewell to Haydn's youth (he was thirty-three), for he never quite recaptured the deep-seated *joie de vivre*, the innocent warmth, of this music.

Esterház and the Advent of Sturm und Drang (1766–74)

After the steady symphonic production of the years 1757/8–65, it is surprising to note that only about ten symphonies, including a lost work in D major listed in Haydn's Draft Catalogue (*Entwurf-Katalog*), were written between 1766 and 1770. The reasons for this sudden decline may be attributed to several outward circumstances.

In 1766, Haydn's predecessor Gregor Werner died, an embittered old man who had been spitefully jealous of his brilliant young assistant. Although Werner's position at the court had been purely nominal for the past few years, it is interesting to note that Haydn wrote practically no church music of any significance in these years, possibly not to offend Werner, who had been in his day a well-known composer of Masses. Haydn was now promoted to full *Kapellmeister*, and with this honour went a number of new responsibilities, such as the production of church music. This very year, 1766, Haydn wrote his first large-scale Mass, the *Missa in honorem B. V. M.*, the next year his famous *Stabat Mater*, the year after that the lost *Missa Sunt bona mixta malis* in D minor; in 1772, the *Missa Sancti Nicolai*, and probably in 1773 the huge *Missa Sanctae Caeciliae*.

In 1766, Prince Nicolaus Esterházy opened Esterház, an elaborate palace erected on the grounds formerly occupied by a modest hunting lodge. In this year, the theatre and various other buildings – including permanent quarters for the musicians – were not yet finished; but in the ensuing years, Esterház was to become the focal point of musical activity for the court. In 1766 Haydn wrote his opera *La canterina* which was given at the big hall in Eisenstadt as a sort of dress rehearsal and the next year at Pressburg (Bratislava). In 1768, the new opera house at Esterház was ready, and Haydn wrote for it the first of his three Goldoni operas: *Lo speziale*. The following year Haydn spent writing his second Goldoni subject, *Le pescatrici*, which has recently been revived at the Holland and Edinburgh Festivals (1965). In the late 1760s Haydn again turned to the quartet, which he had neglected since inventing the form for Fürnberg a decade earlier, and composed Op. 9 – it has been established that Op. 3 is not by Haydn but by *Pater* Romanus Hofstetter, a German monk whose quartets were widely circulated in their day. In 1771, he wrote his Quartets Op. 17, and the next year his celebrated Op. 20.

This brief survey shows that, on becoming full musical director, with the opening of Esterház, Haydn's activities were sufficiently widespread to force the symphony, for the moment, into a secondary rôle. He did not stop composing them – he never did entirely, till after London – but they are less frequent. Although not many autographs of these symphonies exist, we have a chronological aid in Haydn's *Entwurf-Katalog*, which is a running (mostly autograph) list of new works, entered in blocks every few years. By using those works with known dates (*i.e.* where dated manuscripts are extant), we can often date, within a year or two, those works of uncertain chronological position.

1765–66: Symphony No. 34 (earliest reference: 1767).

1766–68: Symphonies Nos. 35 (autograph: 1 December, 1767), 59 (*Entwurf-Katalog*, entered after 35), 38, (next entry in *Entwurf-Katalog*), 49 (next entry: autograph 1768), 58 (next entry), 39 (*Entwurf-Katalog*, pencilled entry at top of p. 2, to left of *Lo speziale* Overture, 1768), 26 (entered in *Entwurf-Katalog* directly after *Lo speziale* Overture of 1768), 41 (the next entry: authentic MS parts in Prague on paper which may be dated 1769), followed by what used to be a lost work, rediscovered in the Library of Congress (Washington) and seen to be the missing Overture to *Le pescatrici*, first performed in 1770. It begins:

EX. 6

Symphony No. 34 is the fifth Haydn symphony in the *sonata da chiesa* form: it opens with a sober D minor *adagio* which is perhaps the first hint of the new style that Haydn gradually began to adopt. The rest of the work is in the tonic (D) major. In the late 1760s and early 1770s, Austrian music began to be swept by a wave of romanticism; the new style has been compared to the similar trend in German literature that takes its name from the play, *Sturm und Drang* (Storm and Stress), by Friedrich Maximilian von Klinger (1752–1831) which, however, follows Symphony No. 34 by some ten years. The romantic plays of this period, which took as their inspiration Shakespeare (German translations of whose plays were commissioned *inter alia* by Prince Nicolaus Esterházy and given by the Wahr troupe at Esterház), produced as profound a stylistic revolution in German literature as did the Austrian movement in music. There seems little doubt, however, that this

Austrian *Sturm und Drang* set in before the German literary movement, and we must doubt a real connection between the two except in vague generalities. Nevertheless it is clear that intellectuals in all spheres of the arts were attempting to purge their respective fields of rococo super-ficialities. With the Austrian musicians this was accompanied by the curious paradox of a return to strict contrapuntal forms which were, in the late 1760s, judged old-fashioned except in the composition of church music. We thus find strict counterpoint playing an ever increasing rôle in the Austrian symphony and quartet of this period: there are fugal movements not only in the quartets of Haydn's Op. 20 but in d'Ordoñez's and Gassmann's quartets. After the swing of the pendulum so far to the left, the style soon steadied itself and composers were concerned with creating forms which could encompass the stricter contrapuntal texture as well as the modern sonata (or variation or rondo) concepts. There is no doubt that Haydn was at the forefront of this new hybrid style, and that the wedding of older forms to newer content is in large measure his achievement. He applied his new principles to the finale of Symphony No. 38, where we find an extraordinary mixture of concerto elements (a solo oboe which suddenly emerges from the orchestra in a brilliant *concertante* passage and later re-enters with flourishes) embedded in sonata form, to which is added a thick contrapuntal texture as the piece progresses.

With Symphony No. 26 (*Lamentatione*) we are in the middle of the new Storm-and-Stress period, and it is characteristic that Haydn should turn to plainsong for the first and second movements. In the opening *allegro assai con spirito* the second subject turns out to be a Passion-tone from the late Middle Ages which was well known to audiences in Haydn's time. (It had been constantly reprinted, up till the 1770s.) The second movement uses the Gregorian chant 'Incipit lamentatio' from the Lamentations of Jeremiah: Haydn had a particular affection for this agelessly beautiful melody, and he had lovingly used it in an early (1760) wind-band divertimento for Count Morzin, and was later to base the trios of Symphonies 45 (*Farewell*) and 80 on it. Mozart later used it for his *Maurerische Trauermusik*. Haydn's Symphony No. 26 ends with a *menuet*, which has led scholars to ponder its original form: can it have been composed as the prelude to some church work? This minuet, with its grim canonic entries and sudden rests is a far cry from dance music.

Symphony No. 39 is another fascinating *Sturm und Drang* piece. It is in G minor and for technical reasons Haydn uses four horns, two in the tonic (G) and two in the relative major (B flat), a procedure which soon was copied by other Austrian composers, including J. B. Vanhal and Mozart (K183). (Mozart also intended K550 to have four horns, but after writing a few bars changed his mind and used only two, one in G and one in B flat). In Haydn's G minor work, we notice several features which are typical of this period: the ferocious concentration of the quick movements, with repeated *tremolo* semiquavers (*cf.* finale); the frequent wide skips in the thematic material (*cf.* the theme of the finale); the effortless introduction of thick contrapuntal passages, wherein the viola now plays a much more important rôle than hitherto (in a letter of 1768, Haydn points out, 'I would ask you to use two players on the viola part throughout, for the inner parts sometimes need to be heard more than the upper parts, and you will find in all my compositions that the viola rarely doubles the bass');[1] the increased use of accents (*fz*); and above all the wide range of emotional contrast within an individual work. Haydn has, in a word, become a mature and profound composer.

This new profundity manifests itself also in works that are not strictly speaking *Sturm und Drang*. As will have been gathered, the use of the minor key is a typical feature of this romantic period: whereas in the Italian baroque, minor keys usually meant festive if dignified *concerti grossi*, for the *Sturm und Drang* composers minor keys were the vehicle for their turbulent thoughts; and thus D minor in *c.* 1770 means something quite different from D minor fifty years before in a Vivaldi concerto. But even in works in the major key, Haydn's new style is often apparent. In the development section of Symphony No. 35/I – a sunny work with a singing main theme – the principal subject develops tiger's claws and becomes ominous and dark-hued. Similarly, the *Fire* Symphony No. 59 – perhaps written as incidental music to some German play – has outbursts of real power and passion (such as the *ff* horn entries in the slow movement); the first movement, with its strange opening 'theme' (which partly consists of repeated notes, first quavers, then semiquavers) and abrupt dynamic contrasts could not have been written for Count Morzin.

Symphony No. 49 (*La Passione*) is the sixth and last of the symphonies written in the church-sonata scheme, with opening slow movement. *La Passione* is a profoundly pessimistic work in F minor in which all four movements remain in the minor: only the trio has a glint of sunlight with its F major and a marvellous horn entry that rises metallically to top f″, but the horns here shine only as gunmetal shines – glinting on a

1 *The Collected Correspondence and London Notebooks of Joseph Haydn* (edited and translated by H. C. Robbins Landon) (London, 1959), p. 10.

grey background. *La Passione* is one of the few apt titles that posterity has given a Haydn symphony: it really might have been a work for Good Friday, and it deeply impressed the musical world of that period (it was written in 1768), for it was widely circulated in manuscript copies (as far as Padua and Spain) and printed in Paris and London.

Two C major Symphonies in Haydn's festive manner were composed in this period – Nos. 38 and 41, both with trumpets and timpani (which Haydn may have added later, for there are authentic manuscripts of both works without them). Of these No. 41 is a clear link to the second part of this period. It is a splendid, large-scale work, with a beautiful slow movement in which a flute appears for the first time: the use of the wind instruments in this *un poco andante* is particularly striking. It was in earlier times the custom to omit the wind instruments from the slow movement, and sometimes (as in No. 39) Haydn still does; but gradually he abandons this early classical habit, and the wind instruments soon contribute a particular colour to the adagios and andantes of these symphonies. In No. 41 the horns are in low C (C *basso*), as opposed to the brilliant high C (C *alto*) of the other movements, and this is in keeping with the dream-like, flowing character of the *andante*.

The first part of the 1770s saw another flowering of Haydn's symphonic output. In these works, the composer's genius reaches hitherto undreamed of heights of grandeur and fantasy. All the promise of the works composed in the late 1760s here reaches fulfilment, and as always in Haydn, a high spiritual level went hand in hand with staggering quantity. The following symphonies were written in the period 1770–74: Nos. 42, 43, 44, 45, 46, 47, 48,[1] 50, 51, 52, 54, 55, 56, 57, 60, 65 and possibly 64 – a total of seventeen works. In these same years we have twelve string quartets (Opp. 17 and 20), half a dozen or more piano sonatas, two Masses (one the enormous *Missa Sanctae Caeciliae*), a *Salve Regina* in G minor, a part of *Le pescatrici* (begun in 1769 but first performed in 1770), the operas *L'infedeltà delusa* (possibly his greatest dramatic work), *Philemon und Baucis, Der Götterrath* and *Hexenschabbas* as well as numerous smaller pieces (baryton trios, etc.). It is almost unbelievable, were it not for almost similar feats by Bach and Mozart and Handel.

In no other symphonies, except in the twelve composed for London and possibly the six for Paris, did Haydn reach the consistently high standard achieved in these seventeen symphonies written in so short a

1   A fresh source for No. 48, very recently discovered in Slovakia, bears the pencilled date 1769.

period. There are indeed some who maintain that he never surpassed the strength and beauty of the *Trauersymphonie* ('Mourning'), the *Farewell,* the G major No. 47, the *Maria Theresa* (No. 48) or the C major No. 56. And when he was an old man, with literally hundreds of compositions to choose from, it is reported that Haydn asked to have the slow movement of the *Trauersymphonie* played at his funeral.

Haydn no longer writes in any one formal pattern, in any one particular style (in the restricted sense); these symphonies offer us every mood imaginable: from the depths of sorrow to angry passion; from the sweetness and infinite wisdom of the adagios to the humorous, flying finales; from witty and popular minuets to the majesty and splendour of the C major symphonies, standing in the shadow of the *Missa Sanctae Caeciliae.* The description given by Mozart to a set of piano concerti might apply to these symphonies of Haydn; for there are parts for the connoisseur (a 'Menuet al Roverso', in which the second group of eight bars is the first group played backwards, note for note – this happens in No. 47/III), as well as parts for Everyman, who will be stirred and uplifted without knowing how or why. Because of this enormous variety, however, one cannot easily lay bare the structure of Haydn's genius merely by pointing out formal characteristics common to all the symphonies concerned (*e.g.* the strong unison openings). Such a movement as No. 47/I, with its terrace-like construction of the main theme and the brilliant inspiration of the recapitulation (wherein the march-like theme enters in the tonic minor and becomes distinctly sinister) is unique among Haydn symphonies.

In several of the works under discussion, there are slow introductions – a device that previously Haydn had employed only in the hybrid symphony No. 25 (No. 15, it will be recalled, starts with a slow-fast-slow movement) and in Nos. 6 and 7. It was noted that with No. 49 (*La Passione*) of 1768 Haydn wrote the last of his *sonata da chiesa* symphonies, with an entire opening slow movement. It must now strike the listener that the slow introduction – once he had abandoned the church-sonata scheme – takes the place of the opening slow movement; the following works have such introductions: Nos. 50, 54 (added later), 57. Gradually Haydn became increasingly fond of the slow introduction, to the point that of twelve London symphonies, only one lacks it.

The freedom and inspiration of Haydn's treatment of sonata form led to some extraordinary results. With No. 45/I – the only symphony in the eighteenth century in F sharp minor – the whole movement seems to be one enormous development section. The second subject is brought in well *after* the double bar, in what would be the normal development section, and never again: it is, incidentally, a strong lyrical contrast to the stormy syncopations of the main subject. The recapitulation, too, is quite irregular in that Haydn continues developing the main theme. This formal freedom is also found in the other three movements. As for the famous finale, it had a programmatic content – the Prince had stayed on too long in Esterház and Haydn thought up an idea to get him to leave: the musicians extinguished their candles and left, one after another, leaving at the end only Haydn and Luigi Tomasini, the leader. Prince Nicolaus is reported to have said, 'Well, if they all leave I suppose we had better leave, too', and accordingly the whole court departed the next day. This ingenious idea has possibly blinded us to the fantastic way in which Haydn breaks off his *presto* (F sharp minor), begins a whole new *adagio* in A major (the relative major) and gradually works the music round, in slow and stately modulations, to the tonic major (F sharp). The score gradually shrinks, leaving at the end only two solo violins – Haydn divided the violins in four for the final *adagio*. In many ways, however, this is unbelievably emotional and high-charged music which must have rocked Prince Nicolaus as much for its general style as for its special message. There is no doubt that, being a practising musician himself and a man of taste, he got the former as well as the more obvious latter.

An equally highly charged work is the *Trauersymphonie*, in E minor, with a contrapuntally extended opening movement and a minuet written as a strict canon between top and bottom lines. In contrast to this are the heavenly slow movement mentioned above and a trio where the cantabile character is both enhanced and paradoxically made tense by having the first horn double the melody in its highest register. By this time, *forzati* often appear all over the page – accents to pinpoint a syncopation, to underline a dissonance, to urge the performers to drive forward an already nervous line. The finale of No. 44 is perhaps the most concentrated and overwhelming *Sturm und Drang* movement Haydn ever wrote: in the development section the tension, and the line, rise in jagged motivic sequences to the point of exhaustion.

The finale of No. 44 is in a kind of monothematic sonata form; in No. 42 Haydn writes a full-scale rondo, wherein the main section (always slightly varied) returns in the characteristic pattern A-B-Á-C-A-Coda. It is a whimsical and amusing movement and the form was one Haydn grew to love dearly; later he combined sonata and rondo forms into a brilliant intellectual exercise (No. 102, for instance).

As the listener will soon perceive, every work is different from its partners. In No. 51 Haydn returns to the divertimento (or if you will, concerto) and writes dazzlingly difficult solo horn parts, not only for the first horn, but using stopped notes (the hand was inserted into the bell of the instrument and the pitch thus lowered) he explores the lowest register of the second horn – this is in the slow movement, where the cantabile character of the theme is specially suited to the horn. The minuet is a delightful trick; the bass repeats itself (four notes) at different intervals throughout, and Haydn joked with his players in that he wrote the four notes only once and then put in changes of clefs for the repetitions. There are two trios (some manuscripts have only the one with the solo horns), which remind one of Bach's Brandenburg Concerto No. 1 (which Haydn doubtless had never even heard of), and the finale is again one of Haydn's new rondos.

In Symphony No. 46, the finale breaks off to re-introduce a large part of the minuet; in the finale of No. 47, we seem, after the placid opening, to be transported into a gipsy camp gone mad. (In Op. 20, No. 4, a quartet written the very same year, 1772, there are also strong Hungarian, or if you will, gipsy elements in the finale.) But there is no end to the variety and originality of this music.

Four glorious C major symphonies with their characteristic C *alto* horn parts, trumpets and kettledrums were written during these years. No. 60 is discussed below. No. 50 (1773) is perhaps a little disappointing, for the slow movement sounds definitely antiquated in orchestration (strings only) and content. But the other movements are worthy of this period, and the minuet is highly original in that the trio is not treated as a separate entity but is joined to the minuet on both sides (Haydn also does this in a fragment of a C major symphony written in these years, the finale of which he later used in Symphony No. 63: *vide infra*). But the two supreme highpoints of Haydn's C major trumpet-symphonies, if we may coin the term, are the *Maria Theresa* (No. 48) and No. 56, the finest of the species until No. 82, written more than ten years later. Both works – though the slow movement of No. 56 is finer than that of *Maria Theresa* – represent a miraculous fusion of various contrasting elements within the realm of festive pomp and splendour; they are indeed music fit for an empress. (No. 48 was apparently played when Maria Theresa visited Esterház in the early autumn of 1773, though it had been composed earlier.)

Symphony No. 54 is the only Haydn symphony before the London ones with the full 'classical' orchestra minus clarinets (which Haydn had

28

for only a few years at Esterház): flutes, oboes, bassoons, horns, trumpets, timpani and strings, whereby the flutes and trumpets (and the slow introduction) were added to the manuscript later. It was also the first work in Haydn's output to use trumpets and drums in G major. (Haydn had to use the trumpets in C, because G would have been too high; later he started to write the *Surprise* Symphony with high G, or 'English', trumpets but gave up after the first movement and resorted to the usual C instruments.) The slow movement of No. 54 carries the delicately balanced, highly emotional type of *adagio* prevalent in this period to its highest degree; it is a very long movement and, because of the concentration it requires (which Haydn makes clear by using the slowest tempo known: *adagio assai*) it is also exhausting, if immensely rewarding. Everything moves with measured and delicate slowness, like an ancient Spanish dance: it is the exact opposite of the near-hysterics generated in such movements as the finale to No. 44, and if we compare these two movements, we see the new range of Haydn's expression. Although Haydn covers the emotional gamut, it is interesting to note that he is able to do so with a small orchestra that rarely, at this period, goes beyond oboes, horns and strings (with a bassoon or two doubling the bass). There are few rules that one can lay down for his symphonies of this epoch, but one instrumental device seems to have utterly fascinated him: the use of mutes for the slow movements. It gives a bitter-sweet, veiled quality to the music which was perhaps necessary to set off the tension and force of the flanking movements.

The fourth C major trumpet-symphony received its public première at the town theatre of Pressburg (Bratislava) on St Cecilia's Day, 1774; it had been composed earlier in the year for the Wahr troupe, who visited Esterház that year for many months, and gave a German translation, *Der Zerstreute*, of Regnard's *Le Distrait*, with new incidental music by Haydn. In a report from Esterház of 30 June, the *Pressburger Zeitung* writes, 'connoisseurs consider this music a masterpiece. It is full of the musical humour, the high spirits and the intelligence which characterize Haydenesque [*sic*] productions. The connoisseurs are amazed on the one hand, whilst on the other the public is simply enchanted, for Hayden [*sic*] knows how to satisfy both parties.' When Wahr gave the piece at Pressburg, the finale of Haydn's music had to be repeated ('upon incessant applause of the audience'). This Symphony No. 60 (known by the Italian name of the play, *Il distratto*) is in six movements, and might be called a medley of folk tunes. In the second movement there is what the Sieber edition calls *ancien chant françois*. In the fourth movement there is a whole string of Hungarian melodies, while in the preceding trio of the minuet there were typical Balkan progressions. In the fifth movement, there is what appears to be a Gregorian chant (in a manuscript at Melk Monastery in Lower Austria the movement is entitled *Adagio di Lamentatione*, but the melody used is not that of the 'Incipit lamentatio' known to us from Symphony No. 45/III and other Haydn pieces). The finale has an uproarious moment when the violins forget that the lowest string is tuned to F instead of G: the music stops and with screeching discords the violins are tuned and the music then races on. 'In this number', writes the *Pressburger Zeitung* after the première at Pressburg, 'which is most effective, allusion is made to the distracted gentleman who, on his wedding day, forgets that he is a bridegroom and has to remind himself by tying a knot in his cravat.' In this finale appears a favourite Balkan tune which Haydn used in a *Cassatio* for clarinets, horns and strings in C (1761), in a divertimento for horns and strings (the original and authentic version of the String Quartet, Op. 2, No. 3), and in the *Il distratto* Symphony:

EX. 7

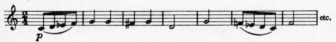

Some years ago the author discovered a curious anonymous eighteenth-century manuscript for violin entitled 'Der Nachtwachter' [*sic*; *sc.* = *Nachtwächter*] ('Night Watchman'), in the library of Metten Monastery (Bavaria).[1] Here the same melody is found in a short piece, with some variations – or if you will, extensions – which show that the tune was well known in southern Europe. With clattering kettledrums and the typical high horns (with optional trumpets) of these C major symphonies, *Il distratto* ends its merry pranks and sums up, in its genuine wit and fascinating variety, all the genius of Haydn in his early forties.

There are, in a survey such as this one, many works which we have had to pass over – though the reader need not pass them over. Symphonies such as the *Mercury* (No. 43, E flat), or the famous *Schoolmaster* (No. 55, with some wonderful moments in the sophisticated and witty slow movement and, as in No. 42, a racy wind-band solo in the finale) – every work of this period had its felicities.

---

1   H. C. Robbins Landon, *Supplement to 'The Symphonies of Joseph Haydn'* (London, 1961), facing p. 32.

The Symphonies of 1775–84

During these ten years, the symphony no longer occupied a central position in Haydn's *oeuvre*; for this was the period when opera began to assume an ever-increasing rôle at Esterház – not only Haydn's own but also those by other composers. A recently published book by two Hungarian scholars, Dénes Bartha and Laszlo Somfai, gives a fascinating picture of Haydn as the director of a complicated opera-house. There were actually two houses, one for the Italian opera and plays, and one for the marionette operas (which were always in German). Haydn not only conducted all the performances, but also supervised the acquisition of the music; as time went on and he became less tolerant of the operatic scores of his (primarily Italian) colleagues, he also arranged, reorchestrated and even recomposed much of the music. He threw out some of the original arias and substituted those of his own. To give one particularly striking example of what this operatic activity at Esterház entailed: in the year 1786 Haydn conducted seventeen operas in 125 performances including eight new productions in the period from 1 March to about 21 December. It is something of a miracle that Haydn could compose anything in 1786, but we know he composed several magnificent symphonies (Nos. 82, 84, 86), six concertos for the *lira organizzata* and several 'insertion' arias.

The chronological list of symphonies written during 1775–84 is:

c. 1775:   No. 64, a work which we have considered as belonging to the previous period.

1776:   No. 61 (dated autograph).

c. 1777–78:   Nos. 53 (second version of finale dated 1777), 63 (first movement based on *Il mondo della luna* overture, 1777).

c. 1778:   Nos. 66–68 (printed by Hummel of Berlin–Amsterdam in 1779; No. 66 in Göttweig Abbey, 1779), No. 69 (Göttweig Abbey, 1779).

1779:   No. 70 (parts in Esterházy Archives dated 18 December 1779).

c. 1780:   Nos. 62 (printed by Hummel in 1782), 71 (MS. in Gesellschaft der Musikfreunde dated 1780, Göttweig Abbey, 1781), 74 (arrived in London in August 1781), 75 (Göttweig, 1781).

1781:   No. 73 (dated autograph).

1782:   Nos. 76–78 (Haydn's letter of 15 July 1783).

1783–84:   Nos. 79–81 (Haydn's letter of 25 October 1784).

On the whole these are not Haydn's best symphonic works: he found himself getting extremely popular, and reports of his success came from as far away as Spain and England. Some of these symphonies seem to have been written for popular consumption, for easy comprehensibility by the masses, and yet there are always some works which would appear to be 'Esterház' productions. Thus an extraordinary work like No. 67, with its use of *col' legno d'arco* (bow turned round and played against the string on the wooden side) and its *two* highly emotional slow movements (one begins with a solo string trio), stands next to No. 66, basically a superficial work despite its supreme craftsmanship. In fact, Haydn never entirely loses his grip, for even in these popular symphonies there are magical moments – thus in the minuet of No. 53 there is a long lead-back which is of extreme beauty and poignancy. The slow movements tend to be themes with variations (the melody of No. 53 appears to be an old French song), while the last movements tend more and more to that swift type of rondo that people evidently loved.

Nos. 61 and 64 are both 'Esterház' symphonies, not for export (curiously: there are not nearly so many contemporary manuscripts of these two works as there are of, say, No. 53 or No. 63): and they both contain marvellous details, particularly in their slow movements. No. 69 is known as the *Laudon*: it is Haydn's own title, to honour the famous Austrian *Feldmarschall* who conquered the Turks and made eastern Europe safe for Austrian monarchism. It is scored for Haydn's usual C major combination, with horns (this time apparently in low C rather than C *alto*), trumpets and kettledrums; but it compares poorly with the breadth and scope of earlier C major symphonies such as Nos. 48 or 56. On the other hand, No. 70, composed just afterwards, is full of remarkable moments. Haydn added the timpani part later, in his own hand, to the manuscript now in the Esterházy archives. This manuscript was written just after a disastrous fire at Esterház which destroyed the opera-house and a great deal of the music; for that reason we only have Haydn's original performance materials for symphonies after the great fire (except, of course, the Fürnberg Collection, which was apparently copied before Haydn entered the service of the Esterházys, and in any case sent 'abroad' – which is why it has survived). The fire can thus date certain manuscripts, such as the original performance material of No. 62, to which Haydn added an autograph flute part for one movement: it must post-date December 1779. The original parts of No. 70 are dated 18 December 1779. The symphony has a most interesting slow movement, a canon in double counterpoint, which means that the top and bottom lines can be inverted. The finale is an adventurous movement which begins in D minor, also the key of the slow movement (the rest of the work is in D major), and contains in the middle a triple fugue of real power.

In the early 1780s, Haydn occasionally experimented with new (for him) dynamic marks: the second movement of No. 74 has a wealth of *crescendi, decrescendi*, accents, and the like. This new dynamic language may have had its origin in the fact that Haydn intended the symphony for export, because when he sent it to Forster in London in the summer of 1781, he seems to have added many of these dynamic marks; they are not found in the earlier Austrian sources. Haydn was always slightly worried about what foreign performers would do to his symphonies, and when sending a manuscript abroad he would often add things – especially accents, *fz* – which he probably explained orally to his own players. Thus authentic parts of Haydn's symphonies often contain dynamic marks not found in the composer's own autographs, and for that reason these parts are, textually, indispensable.

No. 75 is another work to which Haydn seems to have added the trumpets and kettledrums later. By now the slow introduction is becoming much more frequent, and No. 75 begins with a typical short *grave*. Strangely, however, Nos. 76–81 have no slow introductions. No. 75 has a beautiful, hymn-like melody in the slow movement which we shall encounter frequently in the 1780s: the slow movement of No. 88 is a famous example. In connection with the slow movement of No. 75, Haydn wrote down a curious story in his London diary:

On 26th March [1792] at Mr Barthelemon's Concert, an English clergyman was present who fell into the most profound melancholy on hearing the Andante [here Haydn quotes the theme of Symphony No. 75/III] because he had dreamt the previous night that this piece was a premonition of his death. – He left the company at once and took to his bed.

Today, the 25th of April, I heard from Herr Barthelemon that this protestant clergyman had died.

The famous symphony *La Roxelane* (No. 63) seems to have been written as incidental music to a German translation of Favart's *Les trois sultanes* which the Karl Wahr troupe gave at Esterház in 1777. In some respects this work is a typical symphony of its period. For one thing, it shows how involved Haydn was with opera, for the first movement is lifted bodily from the overture to *Il mondo della luna* of that year. The slow movement, a witty double variation (alternating C minor and C major), is entitled 'La Roxelane' after the leading character in the play. For the finale Haydn originally used an earlier (*c.* 1769–73) movement from a fragment of a C major symphony of which only the minuet and finale exist (Berlin State Library, partly in Haydn's handwriting). Later he replaced this lively piece with another in the more popular style. As a result of these borrowings, the orchestration was changed from version to version: for the *Mondo* overture Haydn used a large orchestra, including two oboes, two bassoons, two horns, two trumpets, timpani and strings. For the symphony version, Haydn dropped the trumpets and timpani, dropped one of the two bassoons, and added a flute. In the older symphony fragment there were also trumpets and timpani, which Haydn dropped for *La Roxelane*, but there was no bassoon part at all. As one can see, things were in considerable chaos by the time the symphony began to be circulated, and it seems that Haydn revised the work, so that (for instance) the bassoon had something to do in the finale: for curious as it sounds, the second finale was also composed at first without a bassoon part. In a word, we are dealing with a piece of incidental music which Haydn later whipped into a symphony.

For No. 53 there exist no fewer than four different finales. No. 1 is a curious *capriccio* which is in the manuscript from the Esterházy archives. No. 2 is an overture that Haydn wrote in 1777: the autograph shows that it was intended as an overture, because it modulates to the dominant of C major – the home key is D – and breaks off with a pause. Haydn later cancelled this part when using it as a finale. No. 3 is very dubious and appears in a French print of the time. No. 4, whose autograph was recently discovered in Russia, bears the title 'Finale', and one Italian manuscript of the symphony has in fact this movement as the finale. Haydn published it separately as an overture (Hoboken Ia, 4),[1] but obviously when it was written, he thought of it as a finale. The first three versions are published with the Philharmonia miniature score (No. 593), the fourth version as an overture by Doblinger Verlag. Although the timpani part of the first movement of No. 53 is patently by Haydn, the timpani parts of the third (minuet) and fourth (version No. 1) movements are very curious and may have been added by a pupil.

All this is cited because one cannot escape the impression that in the symphonies of this decade Haydn was working under great pressure and composed these works in rather a hurry, throwing together movements and patching different orchestrations together. An even more curious

1   A. von Hoboken, *Joseph Haydn, Thematisch-bibliographisches Werkverzeichnis* (Mainz).

illustration of this *pasticcio* procedure concerns the second finale of No. 53 (Hoboken Ia, 7). Although Haydn had used it twice, once as an overture and once as a symphonic finale, he now proceeded to use it, with slight alterations, as the opening movement to Symphony No. 62. Another curious point about this symphony is that all four movements are in one key, a procedure that Haydn hitherto had reserved for church-sonata symphonies; in this case, however, it looks as if the other movements (II–IV) were possibly composed for something else – incidental music to a play? – and the first later tacked on. This theory is borne out by examination of the original performing material in the Esterházy archives. The overture had no flute part, and thus in the symphonic version of No. 53, using the overture as finale, the flute simply quits after the third movement. Haydn does not seem to have added a flute for the finale version, though the publisher Hummel apparently did – this is printed in smaller type in the Philharmonia miniature score; but when he came to use it the third time, for the first movement of No. 62, he saw that it would be a little strange if the flute did not start to play until the second movement, and so he added the part himself with the note, 'Friend, look for the first Allegro'. This kind of thing happens all the time in the music of Bach and Handel, but much more rarely in Haydn, and for the most part during these hectic years of operatic productions.

The shadow of the opera-house at Esterház also hangs heavy over Symphony No. 73 (*La Chasse*), the last movement of which was originally (1780) the overture to Haydn's opera, *La fedeltà premiata*. It had trumpets and drums, and in this case Haydn left the instruments in the symphonic version, so that they first appear in the finale. When the work was published by Torricella in Vienna, these instruments were omitted; but the earliest manuscripts and the French edition of Sieber include them, and they add a touch of drama and colour to an otherwise rather unremarkable work. The *pasticcio* nature of Haydn's symphonies in these years is further revealed by the origin of the slow movement in No. 73, which was originally a song called 'Gegenliebe' which Haydn wrote the same year as the symphony, 1781.

On 15 July 1783 Haydn wrote to a French publisher named Boyer: 'Last year I composed three beautiful, elegant and by no means over-lengthy symphonies. . . . They are all very easy, and without too much *concertante*.' By now Haydn was well connected with several publishing houses: Artaria in Vienna, Forster in London, and two or three in Paris, to whom he sold symphonies and chamber music. He got into trouble with Forster for selling him 'exclusive' rights to works which Haydn also sold to Artaria, who promptly sent their copies to their London agents, Longman & Broderip. Forster later sued Haydn when the latter was in London, but the matter appears to have been settled out of court. Up to 1780, Haydn's principal method of securing subsidiary rights was to sell manuscript copies of his music to princely courts, monasteries, and so forth; he supervised these copies, using several Viennese copyists and copying firms. But after 1780 he gradually saw that more money, and a wider distribution, could be had by having his music published. By this time, moreover, he must have learned to his chagrin that French, German and English publishers had been selling pirated editions of his music, from the sale of which the composer never made a penny. It was a very cut-throat, dog-eat-dog relationship, that of composer and publisher; and Haydn felt no more compunction in selling the same piece to three publishers (as he did with Symphonies 76–78 – to Artaria, Boyer and Forster) than they did in securing pirated copies of his music from which to engrave.

In the above letter to Boyer, Haydn tells the French publisher that the symphonies had been intended for England, but that the journey had failed to materialize. It was the London opera that had wanted to engage Haydn, as we know from a letter Charles Burney wrote about this time to his friend the Rev. Thomas Twining; we do not know why the contract was not made. In any case, this is the first evidence that Haydn was now thinking of symphonies in sets. All the remaining symphonies of his life were composed in sets, from pairs (Nos. 88, 89) to sets of six (the two sets of 'Salomon' Symphonies, for instance). It was a typically eighteenth-century concept and one closely bound up with the advent of printed music on a large scale: for publishers loved to issue music in sets, 'Trois Sonates pour le Clavecin ou Piano Forte', or 'Sei Sinfonie per grande orchestra' or 'Six Quartettos for two Violins, a Tenor, and a Violoncello, as performed at the Professional Concert'. It is significant that apart from Nos. 6–8, there are no 'sets' of Haydn symphonies prior to 1782 (Nos. 76–78), when for the first time Haydn began to think in terms of publication as well as the immediate composition.

Of the three symphonies intended for London in 1782, No. 77 is the finest – indeed, it is one of the best works of this whole period. There is a spectacular contrapuntal passage in the development of the opening movement, and the finale, too, is one of the first, and at once highly successful, examples of the sonata-rondo form which

Haydn invented. The rondo, in its typical form, is A-B-A-C-A, and to put the matter at its most simple, what Haydn did was to convert the C section into a development section *à la* sonata form, using material from the A section: in this case the main theme. The slow movement, with its intensely concentrated lyricism, is also one of the loveliest of the period. It is the kind of music by Haydn that Mozart, who had just moved to Vienna the year before, must have studied and assimilated.

Mozart and Haydn were to become fast friends; there were no other composers on the Continent at that time to compare in quality with either. In Vienna, then as now a scandal-mongering town with waspish critics and frivolous audiences, Haydn often had to defend his young friend, just as Mozart was constantly defending Haydn from the attacks of Viennese Philistines. In 1785 Mozart invited Haydn to his elegant flat in Vienna, near the Cathedral, to hear the quartets which he lovingly and modestly dedicated to his older friend; and on one such occasion Haydn said to Wolfgang's father, Leopold: 'Your son is the greatest composer I know, either personally or by reputation.' Someone once said that among the Viennese only Haydn, a few of Mozart's personal friends such as the banker Michael Puchberg (also a friend of Haydn's), and possibly the stiff Baron Van Swieten, at whose lodgings Mozart often gave Sunday morning concerts, understood the genius of Mozart. And Haydn often said, 'I had to go to England to become famous in my own country'. In many respects, Haydn was far better off in the wilds of Esterház than was Mozart in the sophisticated atmosphere of Vienna, where he could become a darling of society in a few years only to be ignored and half-forgotten soon afterwards. In 1788 Mozart wrote to Puchberg that he had sent round a subscription list and it had come back with one name only, Van Swieten's; three years earlier the flower of Viennese nobility and the Emperor Joseph II himself had thronged to his concerts. And so, when Haydn sometimes lamented to his friends, 'my trouble is that I live in the country', another voice inside him admitted that 'in Esterház there was no one to confuse or torment me, and I was forced to become original'.

In 1783 and 1784, Haydn composed another set of three symphonies, for what occasion we do not know: possibly he wrote them with an eye primarily to their swift publication. They were finished by the autumn of 1784, and there is a very interesting letter to Haydn's publisher Artaria in which something of Haydn's sense of responsibility towards Prince Nicolaus Esterházy is revealed:

Estoras [*sic*], 20 November 1784

Dearest Friend!

Don't be angry with me that I cannot fulfil any of your wants just now; the 3rd Symphony [Artaria published them in the order 81, 80, 79] is now ready, but you cannot have it before my arrival in Vienna because of some small profit which I shall try to make on all three. The main difficulty in everything is the long sojourn of my Prince in Estoras, even though he doesn't have much to amuse him, since half the theatre is sick or away. So you can imagine what trouble I constantly have to amuse him. . . .

Symphony No. 80 is in many ways a striking work, in D minor, with a spirited opening movement, a songful *adagio* in B flat, and a most extraordinary trio which has a melody that sounds like the inversion of our old friend, the Gregorian 'Incipit lamentatio'. The finale is an amusing and beautifully constructed movement in which the whole impetus is derived from syncopations. These syncopations are so constructed that it is not at once apparent that they *are* syncopations, and so the whole thing is a joke on the audience. No. 81 has a marvellous beginning and is altogether a very sophisticated work: there are distinctly Mozartean touches in the second theme of the opening movement, which winds in a chromatic line reminscent of the Salzburg master. On the whole, however, scholars have vastly overrated the *musical* influence, especially in such technical matters, of Mozart on Haydn and *vice versa*. This is mainly because in the nineteenth and first half of the twentieth centuries most musicians had a much more thorough knowledge of Mozart than of Haydn, with the obvious result that their attempt to show cross-influences between the two masters has been hindered by an imperfect acquaintance with Haydn's *oeuvre*. Mozart learned from Haydn primarily the intellectual approach to sonata form, and since an abstract concept such as this is easily transmutable into a different style, it is no surprise that Mozart's 'Haydn' Quartets – the ones dedicated to the older composer – were able to adopt Haydn's principles but to sound completely Mozartean. Similarly, Mozart's influence on Haydn was not what the textbooks tell us; it was more negative than positive; for instance, when he saw that Mozart was developing a new kind of piano concerto, Haydn, after the D major Concerto published in 1784 (but composed perhaps as early as *c.* 1780), wrote no more works in that form. Similarly, apart from *L'anima del filosofo* (*Orfeo ed Euridice*) which was commissioned by Sir John Gallini for London in 1791, Haydn wrote no more operas after *Armida* (1784). Conversely, he performed *Le nozze di Figaro* at Esterház in 1790. And three years before that, when some-one in Prague had asked him for a new opera, he had written, '. . . I should be risking a great deal, for scarcely any man can brook compari-son with the great Mozart' and went on for the rest of the letter about Mozart's talents — 'how inimitable are Mozart's works, how profound, how musically intelligent, how extraordinarily sensitive! (for this is how I understand them, how I feel them) — why then the nations would vie with each other to possess such a jewel within their frontiers . . .'. It is in fact rather striking to see how *un*-Mozartean Haydn's works after, say, 1785 are; no more Mozartean than Mozart's are Haydnesque. There are exceptions in both cases, as I have pointed out with No. 81, but they remain exceptions. For both men's styles were too personal, too distinct to need more than fleeting influence from outside, once each had estab-lished his own, mature language. Of course Mozart was fascinated by Bach's fugues in the early 1780s, and Haydn was equally fascinated by Handel's oratorios in London: but when Mozart came to write his great fugues, such as the Adagio and Fugue in C minor (K546) or the finale of the *Jupiter* Symphony, they were Mozartean and not Bachian fugues; and when Haydn came to write his great oratorios, *The Creation* and *The Seasons*, they were Haydnesque oratorios, not Handelian.

This section ends, then, with Symphonies Nos. 79–81. *In toto*, it had not been a satisfactory period for the Haydn symphony. Despite some wonderful works and great moments within individual pieces, Haydn did not, in 1775–84, give his best to the symphonic form. In 1784, however, came a flattering commission from Paris which was to affect sharply and swiftly the course of the Haydn symphony, and to place it once again at the forefront of his creative life.

The Paris Symphonies (1785–6);
The Tost Symphonies (1787);
The Symphonies for Comte D'Ogny (1788–9)[1]

We owe the existence of Haydn's famous 'Paris' Symphonies (Nos. 82–87) to a remarkable French aristocrat: Claude-François-Marie Rigoley, Comte d'Ogny (1757–90), one of the backers of the celebrated Parisian concert organization, 'Le Concert de la Loge olympique'.

Haydn's music was, of course, very popular in France long before the advent of the Loge olympique; as early as 1764, Haydn's symphonies and quartets began to be printed in Paris, and the composer himself relates, in a letter to his Viennese publisher Artaria, dated 27 May 1781, that Joseph Le Gros, director of the Concert spirituel, 'wrote me the most flattering things about my *Stabat Mater*, which was performed [in Paris] four times with the greatest applause . . .'. All during the 1780s Haydn's symphonies were performed at the various Parisian concerts with unvarying success, and numerous publishing houses issued every new symphonic work by Haydn they could lay their hands on.

Thus it was natural that the young Comte d'Ogny – he was still in his twenties – as well as the musicians of the Loge olympique should have wanted to commission six symphonies from one of Europe's most popular composers. Since d'Ogny plays such an important rôle in Haydn's Parisian dealings – it was 'Pour S. Excellence' that the composer also wrote Symphonies Nos. 90–92 – a few words about his life may not be amiss here. D'Ogny was born at Dijon in September 1757, the second child of Claude-Jean Rigoley, baron d'Ogny, and Elisabeth d'Alencé (the title of count comes from his mother's side). The family was an old and respected one, whose history can be traced back to the fifteenth century. D'Ogny's father was *Intendant Général des Postes*, a position which his son inherited in 1785; Ogny *père* was also a backer of the Concert des Amateurs, and apparently music played an important part in the family life. The now famous *Catalogue de la Musique de Monsieur Le Comte d'Ogny* (British Museum) shows that the count owned, to quote Barry Brook who discovered the catalogue, 'une des plus riches collections musicales privées qui aient jamais rassemblées au XVIIIᵉ siècle'.[2]

1 I have taken the material for this section largely from my own prefaces to the Philharmonia scores, Vol IX (Nos. 82–87) and Vol. X (Nos. 88–92 and *Concertante*, which will be discussed in the subsequent section).
2 See B. Brook, *La Symphonie française dans la seconde moitié du XVIIIᵉ siècle* (Paris, 1962).

The correspondence between the Concert de la Loge olympique and Haydn has not, unfortunately, survived. It seems that the Comte d'Ogny asked the *chef d'orchestre*, Chevalier Joseph-Boulogne de Saint-Georges – himself a prolific composer – to write to Haydn and settle the details. The Concert agreed to pay Haydn twenty-five louis d'or for each of the six symphonies, 'ce qui avait paru à Haydn un prix colossal, car jusqu'alors ses symphonies ne lui avaient rien rapporté', and a further five louis d'or for the right to publish the new symphonies in Paris.

Haydn wrote two of the symphonies (Nos. 83 and 87), and possibly a third (No. 85), in 1785, and three (Nos. 82, 84, 86) in 1786. The autographs of five have survived, and all appear once to have belonged to the music library of the Comte d'Ogny, for there is a note, on the title-page of the autograph of Symphony No. 82, to the effect that the manuscript was sold at 'la vente du feu Cte d'ogni le 10 février 1791'. The count had died on 4 October 1790, leaving 100,000 livres in debts.

Parisian orchestras of the period were much larger than those of the Austrian and German provincial courts, much larger, too, than Haydn's own modest band at Esterház. The Concert de la Loge olympique, 'rempli indépendamment des professeurs par les plus habiles amateurs de Paris', boasted some forty violins and ten double-basses. The musicians wore splendid sky-blue dress-coats with elaborate lace ruffles, and swords at their sides. The Salle de Spectacle de la Société Olympique was a large theatre with boxes in tiers. The concerts were patronized by the nobility; and Marie Antoinette found the B flat Symphony (No. 85) her favourite – the first edition by Imbault in Paris actually printed the work with the subtitle, *La Reine de France*, under which name the symphony is still known today.

The first performances of the 'Paris' Symphonies appear to have taken place in the season of 1787; the young Cherubini was among the violinists, and later described the rapture with which the best musicians in Paris took part in these premières. The audiences and critics were equally enchanted, and when the new symphonies were played in the Concert spirituel, the critic of the *Mercure de France* wrote:

. . . On a executé à tous les Concerts [l'année dernière] des Symphonies de M. Haydn. Chacque jour on sent mieux, & par conséquent on admire davantage les productions de ce vaste génie, qui, dans chacun de ses morceaux, fait si bien, d'un sujet unique, tirer les développmens si riches & si variés; bien différent des ces Compositeurs stériles, qui passent continuellement d'une idée à l'autre, faute d'en savoir présenter une sous des formes variées, & entassent mécaniquement des effets sur des effets, sans liaison & sans goût. Les Symphonies de M. Haydn, toujours sûres de leur effet, en produiroient encore davantage, si la salle étoit plus sonore. . . .

In January 1788, the *Mercure de France* printed the proud announcement of the Parisian music publisher Imbault, who advertised for sale the six new works. 'Ces Symphonies', continues the notice, 'du plus beau caractère & d'une facture étonnante, ne peuvent manquer d'être recherchées avec le plus vif empressement par ceux qui ont eu le bonheur de les entendre, & même par ceux qui ne les connoisent pas. Le nom d'Haydn répond de leur mérite extraordinaire.'

Meanwhile Haydn sold the works to his Viennese publisher Artaria, and to the British firm of Forster. As readers will have by now realized, the chronology of Symphonies Nos. 82–87 is in any case incorrect. (When the list of Haydn symphonies was made, the existence of the dated autographs of Nos. 83 and 87 was not known.) Haydn wrote to Artaria on 2 August 1787: 'I forgot last time to put down the order of the symphonies, which must be engraved as follows', and specifies the sequence Nos. 87, 85, 83, 84, 86, 82. The Imbault numbering, which may actually represent the order in which the works were sent by Haydn, is: 83, 87, 85, 82, 86, 84. Thus in both cases the known 1785 works (Nos. 83, 87) precede the known 1786 works (Nos. 82, 84, 86), and there seems a certain justification for assuming that No. 85 was composed in 1785 rather than 1786.

It is quite obvious that Haydn wrote most of these symphonies with the Parisian orchestra – reports of whose size and virtuoso standards must surely have reached Esterház – and the French audience in mind. The second movement of No. 85 is based on an old French folk-song, 'La gentille et jeune Lisette,' and it is not 'reading things into the music' to regard the stately minuet of No. 82 as a tribute to pre-Revolutionary Parisian elegance: this *is* a French minuet, one feels.

The 'Paris' Symphonies are a remarkable fusion of brilliance, elegance, and warmth. The emotional range is the biggest in Haydn's symphonies since the *Sturm und Drang* period; we move from the strange and subdued *capriccio* of No. 86/II to the aggressive, timpani-dominated hardness and excitement of No. 82/I. Students of Haydn will notice the great attention to woodwind in these scores – a tribute to the French orchestra, perhaps? – which is seen most strikingly in the long windband solo at the end of No. 84/II, but equally beautifully in No. 83's slow movement, where there are moments (*cf.* bars 64*ff.*) of almost unbearable poignancy.

Formally, Haydn's 'Paris' Symphonies show the composer at his most expansive and inventive. We would point to two great innovations: the minuet of No. 86, wherein the tripartite division clearly takes on the formal and psychological attributes of sonata form (thus bars 1–12 might be considered the exposition, 13–38 the development, using the grace-note figure of bars 1*ff.*, 39–50 the recapitulation and 51–62 the coda); and secondly, the brilliant combination of sonata and rondo forms in the finale of No. 85 – this 'sonata rondo' is a peculiarly Haydn-esque invention which we have noted in connection with Symphony No. 77/IV, and one that allows his constantly increasing attention to the development section to flower within the more restricted channels of the rondo form. Truly, these 'Paris' Symphonies are 'd'une facture étonnante'.

On 22 September 1788, Haydn wrote to his Viennese publisher Artaria:

Monsieur et mon tres [sic] cher Amy
A few days ago I was told that you, my dear Sir, were supposed to have purchased from Herr Tost my very newest 6 Quartets and 2 new Symphonies. Since I would like to know, for various reasons, if this is true or not, I would ask you to let me know on the next post-day. I remain [&c].

With this letter, the story of the curious *affaire* Tost is opened at least as far as the relevant documents have been preserved. Johann Tost was one of the violinists in the Esterházy band, and about this time he decided to go to Paris and seek his fortune there. He took with him several of Haydn's latest works, the Quartets Opp. 54 and 55 and Symphonies Nos. 88 and 89. Obviously Tost had the rights of publication in these works, and Haydn never, in the extant correspondence, doubts these rights; but the composer had apparently not yet received the money Tost had promised him and was thus anxious to know whether Tost had sold the symphonies or not. A little later, on 5 April 1789, Haydn writes to the French publisher Jean-Georges Sieber, who (said Haydn) was supposed to have bought six pianoforte sonatas and four (!) symphonies from Tost. 'Herr Tost has no rights at all to the six piano-forte sonatas and has thus swindled you,' writes Haydn, and adds that Tost 'still owes me 300 Gulden'. 'Now I would ask you,' continues Haydn, 'to tell me candidly just how, and in what fashion, Herr Tost behaved in Paris. Did he have an *Amour* there? And did he also sell you the 6 Quartets, and for what sum?'

Sieber did in fact purchase the new symphonies (Nos. 88 and 89), but Tost also seems to have sold him – as a work of Haydn's – the G major Symphony by Adalbert Gyrowetz, which Sieber brought out under Haydn's name, and which caused poor Gyrowetz, when he shortly afterwards arrived in Paris, a good deal of difficulty inasmuch as no one would believe that Gyrowetz had actually written the symphony.

Tost seems to have been a clever if obviously unscrupulous gentleman, for on 5 July 1789, we find Haydn writing to Artaria:

> Now I would like to know the truth about something: that is, from whom you procured the 2 new symphonies which you recently announced – whether you purchased them from Herr Tost or whether you got them already engraved from Herr Sieber in Paris. If you purchased them from Herr Tost, I beg you to furnish me at once with an *a parte* written assurance of the fact, because I am told that Herr Tost pretends that I sold these 2 symphonies to you and thereby caused him a great loss.

However involved the relations between Artaria, Sieber, Tost and Haydn seem to have been in the summer of 1789, it seems that the *affaire* Tost had a happy end; for Johann Tost returned to Vienna shortly afterwards, where he married Prince Esterházy's housekeeper. Now a rich man, Tost continued to request works from Haydn, and the six Quartets of Op. 64, written in 1790, were dedicated to Tost. Mozart, too, wrote many of his string quintets for Tost, who was now no longer a professional violinist but a wholesale merchant. There is a curious and fascinating chapter about Johann Tost in Spohr's autobiography.

At any rate we owe the existence of Symphonies Nos. 88 and 89 to this interesting, if rather shadowy, figure. No. 88 in G is rightfully one of the most famous and beloved of all Haydn's works: in England it is known as *Letter V* and in Germany *mit dem Dudelsack*, because of the bizarre, bagpipe-like effect of the trio. The *Allgemeine Musikalische Zeitung* (5 December 1798) later referred to the originality of Haydn's use of trumpets and drums in the slow movements of his symphonies – nowadays, writes the paper, an everyday occurrence. Of this slow movement Brahms said, 'I want my Ninth Symphony to sound like this'. The finale is one of the most intricately contrived, yet brilliant sounding, movements Haydn ever composed: a sonata rondo which is a perfect tribute to the Viennese predilection for combining intellect and beauty. Notice in the development section how, after returning, rondo-like, to the tonic key, Haydn suddenly launches into a *fortissimo* canon between upper and lower strings which continues, before our fascinated eyes and delighted ears, bar after bar: surely this is one of the great contrapuntal *tours de force* of the Viennese classical symphony.

Symphony No. 89, placed beside the glowing strength of No. 88, seems at first glance a rather pale companion. No. 89 is reserved, cool and of immaculate formal design, rather like the perfectly fashioned German porcelain figurines of that period; it is often said that Haydn opened the door to the eighteenth-century salon and let in the fresh air; no doubt this is on the whole true, but for No. 89 he momentarily closed the doors again. The slow movement and finale were borrowed from the Concerto No. 5 for the King of Naples, composed a year earlier. Haydn retains the slow movement more or less unchanged, but he enlarged the finale with the highly symphonic section in F minor, whose rather ferocious off-beat *forzati* add strength and orchestral colour to an otherwise rococo movement.

One of Haydn's many foreign patrons was Krafft-Ernst, Prince of Oettingen-Wallerstein, who maintained a famous orchestra in his pretty castle at Wallerstein in south Germany. On 3 February 1788, Haydn writes to the Prince's agent in Vienna, and thanks him for all the compliments which the Prince paid Haydn, but regrets that he has not the time to compose the three new symphonies which the prince would like to have. The princely agent continued to urge Haydn to write these three symphonies, however, and circumstances soon enabled the prince to get the works after all.

The circumstances came from Paris. Encouraged by the sensational success of the 'Paris' Symphonies, Comte d'Ogny urged Haydn to compose three more symphonies for Paris. Haydn, always an astute businessman, decided to satisfy both Prince Krafft-Ernst and Comte d'Ogny; he wrote two in 1788 (Nos. 90 and 91) and one in 1789 (No. 92), dedicating Nos. 91 and 92 personally to M. le Comte d'Ogny. Having sent off the scores to Paris, where Le Duc subsequently engraved the parts ('Du Répertoire de la Loge olympique'), Haydn was left without the autograph manuscripts; and thus he was forced to send orchestral parts to Prince Krafft-Ernst. He posted them to the princely agent in Vienna in the middle of October 1789; the prince seems to have objected because he had not received the autograph scores, to which Haydn replied, in a letter to the agent, that his eyesight was bad and the scores almost illegible. He sent a specimen page to prove his point. The prince also found out that he was not the sole owner of the three works, and maintained that Herr von Kees (a friend and patron of Haydn's in Vienna) also had copies – which was true, because the copies Kees owned still exist in the Thurn und Taxis Library at Regensburg. The agent, however, was convinced of Haydn's innocence and seems to have persuaded the prince that Haydn had acted in good faith. And the prince, obviously a generous man, asked his agent to write to 'Haiden' and order three more symphonies and to invite him to come to Wallerstein at the prince's expense to conduct them. To make the offer more attractive, he sent Haydn a gold snuff-box weighing the value of thirty-four ducats, with another fifty ducats in cash. The agent wrote to the prince on 9 February 1790: '. . . je lui ai écrit, pourqu'il m'assigne une personne, à qui je pouvais confier le Tabatière d'or avec les 50 Ducats, affin qu'ils lui parviennent . . . et lui ai proposé de faire un tour à Wallerstein aux frais de Votre Altesse, qui souhaiteroit faire le connoissance personelle . . .'

As matters turned out, Haydn did visit Wallerstein; for when Prince Nicolaus Esterházy died that year (1790) and Johann Peter Salomon came to Vienna to fetch Haydn to London, the two men travelled *via* the Oettingen-Wallerstein court. There was no time, in December 1790, for a long visit, but a contemporary document from the Oettingen-Wallerstein archives notes that Haydn promised to return on his way back to Austria. We do not know whether Haydn found the time to visit Wallerstein again, but we do know that he delivered to the prince four of the first set of Salomon Symphonies (Nos. 93, 96–98) in manuscript copies which are still extant.

The three Symphonies Nos. 90–92 are the last works in the form written before the London journey. Of them, No. 92 (whose name, the *Oxford*, was given it when Haydn conducted it at the Sheldonian Theatre on the occasion of his receiving the degree of Doctor of Music *honoris causa* in July 1791) is by far the finest. It seems to sum up, to round off, the enormous number of symphonies Haydn had written up to this point; it is a work written in the high summer of a long and productive life, and its infinitely subtle introduction and poetic slow movement show us more of Haydn's true character than do any of his letters of the period. Together with some of the 'Paris' works and No. 88, it is one of the few symphonic works of the time worthy to stand beside the last symphonies of Mozart. No. 90 is distinguished by a number of interesting formal details, for instance the device of uniting the opening slow introduction directly with the ensuing *allegro assai*. The minuet, like that of No. 82, seems to have a particularly stately, French character. Both Nos. 82 and 90 are C major 'trumpet' symphonies, nearly the end of a long and distinguished line of such works which was to conclude with the greatest of them all, No. 97 (written in London). The faint suggestion of courtly superficiality present in No. 90 is not echoed in No. 91 which, though the slow sections do not reach the heavenly serenity of No. 92, is a striking work all the same. Haydn seems to have added the trumpet and drum parts to both Nos. 90 and 92 after having completed the scores. Incidentally, the autograph of No. 92 was not rediscovered until 1956; it had been bequeathed to the Bibliothèque nationale in Paris.

Haydn's quiet life was now suddenly to change. With Esterházy's death in 1790, Haydn was free to travel, though he retained, under his new prince, Anton, the nominal title of *Kapellmeister* and a handsome pension; but Anton disbanded the orchestra and there was no reason for Haydn to stay at Esterház. He went immediately to Vienna. There was soon a flattering offer to pay a visit to the King of Naples, and another from Prince Grassalkovics, who had long admired the composer. The news of Prince Nicolaus's death reached Cologne at a time when Johann Peter Salomon, a German-born violinist who had gone to London to become a leading *impresario*, happened to be on the Continent looking for singers for his next concert season in London. Salomon immediately went to Vienna and strode into Haydn's rooms one morning with the famous sentence, 'I am Salomon of London; I have come to fetch you to England; tomorrow we will make an *accord*', a pun which seems to have delighted Haydn. Mozart, whom Salomon also intended to engage, said to his older friend, 'How will you manage in London? You don't even speak the language.' 'Ah,' said Haydn, 'my language is understood all over the world.' The two friends wept when they parted, and Mozart, with a sudden premonition of the future, cried, 'We shan't ever meet again'. In the middle of December, Haydn and Salomon left for London, where they arrived the day after New Year, 1791.

The 'Salomon' Symphonies
(London, 1791–5)

On 8 January 1791, Haydn wrote from London to his friend, Marianna von Genzinger:

> [After the tiring journey] I am fresh and well again, and occupied in looking at this endlessly huge city of London, whose various beauties and marvels quite astonished me. I immediately paid the necessary calls, such as to the Neapolitan Ambassador and to our own [Austrian]; both called on me in return two days later, and four days ago I lunched with the former – N.B. at 6 o'clock in the evening, as is the custom here.
>
> My arrival caused a great sensation throughout the whole city, and I went the rounds of all the newspapers for three successive days. Everyone wants to know me. I had to dine out six times up to now, and if I wanted, I could dine out every day; but first I must consider my health, and second my work. Except for the nobility, I admit no callers till two in the afternoon, and at four o'clock I dine at home with Mr Salomon. . . . Everything is terribly expensive here . . . I wished I could fly for a time to Vienna, to have more quiet in which to work, for the noise that the common people make as they sell their wares in the street is intolerable. At present I am working on symphonies . . .

Salomon's concert series opened on 11 March 1791 at the Hanover Square Rooms. The new Haydn symphony was No. 96 in D – the chronology of the Salomon symphonies also requires correction – and it was placed at the beginning of the second part, so that the company, some of whom invariably arrived late, could have time to settle down and concentrate on the new piece. A contemporary diary tells us something of the atmosphere that first night:

> . . . The orchestra was arranged on a new plan. The pianoforte [from which Haydn conducted] was in the centre, at each extreme end the double basses, then on each side two violoncellos, then two tenors or violas and two violins, and in the hollow of the piano a desk on a high platform for Salomon with his ripieno. At the back, verging down to a point at each end, all these instruments were doubled, giving the requisite number for a full orchestra. Still further back, raised high up, were the drums, and on either side the

trumpets . . ., bassoons, oboes, clarinets, flutes &c., in numbers according to the requirements of the symphonies. . . . Now the anxious moment arrived, and Salomon having called 'attention' with his bow, the company rose to a person and stood through the whole of the first movement . . . Salomon was wound up to a pitch of enthusiasm beyond himself . . .

The newspapers were equally enthusiastic. The *Diary* wrote that 'the audience was so enraptured, that by unanimous desire, the second movement was encored, and the third was vehemently demanded a second time also, but the modesty of the Composer prevailed too strongly to admit a repetition'.

All sorts of things about *fin de siècle* London concert life must have fascinated Haydn. For one thing, it was the first time that he was writing music directly for a paying audience, so that it was their approval or disapproval — not that of a Prince Esterházy — that determined the success or failure of a given work: for another, there was a large Press, printing daily music criticism, something that did not exist on the Continent. The orchestra was about forty strong, nearly twice as big as Haydn's band at Esterház, and obviously Salomon was a greater musician than Luigi Tomasini, the leader at Esterház. It was also the custom, as we see from the *Diary's* notice, for the audience to register its approval after each individual movement: this led to Haydn's ending slow movements with *forte* chords where one would often expect a soft conclusion, *e.g.* in Symphony No. 97/II. He at first ended Symphony No. 101/II with a loud chord but later cancelled it and replaced it by the soft ending we know today.

The excitement, and the large sums of money Haydn soon began to earn apart from that which he contractually expected from Salomon, soon persuaded him to stay for a second season. As the winter passed to spring and early summer, the Salomon concerts became ever more successful. Haydn had brought with him a lot of his latest music not yet known in England, such as the Quartets Op. 64, Symphonies 90 and 92, and the *Notturni* for the King of Naples; and with all these new pieces, he only had to compose two new symphonies for the first season, Nos. 96 and 95 (they were written in that order). No. 96 is known as the *Miracle* because it was said that a heavy chandelier fell at the first performance and, by a miracle, no one was injured; but in fact contemporary newspapers tell us that the chandelier fell during the performance of Symphony No. 102 in the year 1795.

No. 96 is nevertheless a miracle of sophistication, wit, beautiful orchestration, and charm. The second movement, to which the trumpets and kettledrums contribute a dramatic effect when they enter in the minor section, shows off the London wind players and also contains a particularly beautiful cadenza – just as if the movement were from a concerto – using among other things two solo violins, which weave a gently running pattern through the rich texture of the full band. The minuet is a stirring movement with almost march-like grandeur, while the trio is an Austrian waltz for solo oboe and strings – no wonder the London audiences wanted to have it repeated at the first performance. The symphony is flanked by two elegant movements: the first has a stately slow introduction followed by a scintillating *allegro*, while the last, which Haydn wanted to be played '*pianissimo* and as fast as possible', is a racy and brilliant rondo with all sorts of diversions (an angry section in the minor, a section for the wind band alone, including soft trumpets and drums). There is no possible doubt that the heady atmosphere of London found its way into this gay, bright and deliciously extrovert music. Yet in its quieter moments, No. 96 has something of the lyrical, intimate character of the symphonies of 1788 (particularly the *Oxford*, No. 92).

No. 95 is the only London symphony without a slow introduction: it begins at once with a strong unison figure reminiscent of the *Sturm und Drang* period twenty years earlier. It is also the only London symphony in a minor key. After a powerful and well unified opening movement, the *andante*, a theme and variations in the relative major (E flat), seems a little placid. But the minuet is a very striking movement, using the same dramatic silences that distinguished the first movement; the trio is a virtuoso piece for the solo cello. The finale is the biggest fugal movement of the late symphonies; it is not a strict fugue but, like Mozart's *Jupiter* Symphony, a combination of fugue and sonata, whereby the fugue fulfils, in Haydn's work, something of the psychological nature of the development section in that the fugue's subject is also the principal tune. It is a brilliant and highly successful finale; though the minuet is in the tonic minor, the finale is in C major and lends an optimistic and confident conclusion to Haydn's last symphony in a minor key.

Haydn made many friends in England, and he used the summers to visit them on their country estates. But before he went on holiday, Haydn was given the highest academic honour England could bestow on him – that of doctor of music, *honoris causa*, at Oxford University. The ceremony took place in early July 1791, and Haydn conducted his Symphony No. 92, afterwards known as the *Oxford*, in the Sheldonian. 'I felt very silly in my gown', related Haydn; but he was very proud of his degree.

In August he lunched 'on an East Indian merchant ship with six cannon. I was wonderfully served. . . . In this same month I accompanied Mr Fraser [on a boating party] on the Thames, from Westminster Bridge to Richmond, where we supped on an island; we were twenty-four persons and a wind band.' That month Haydn paid a long visit to friends in Hertfordshire. Later he wrote to Marianna von Genzinger, 'For the last two months I have been living in the country, amid the loveliest scenery, with a banker's family where the atmosphere is like that of the Genzinger family, and where I live as if I were in a monastery. . . . I work hard, and when in the early mornings I walk in the woods alone, with my English grammar, I think of my Creator, my family and all the friends I have left behind – and of these you are the ones I most value. . . . Oh, my dear, gracious lady! How sweet this bit of liberty really is! I had a kind Prince, but sometimes I was forced to be dependent on base souls. I often sighed for release, and now I have it in some measure. . . .' It was certainly at Hertfordshire that Haydn wrote most of Symphonies 93 and 94.

In the autumn Haydn was entertained by the Duke of York on his country estate. The Prince of Wales – later George IV (Haydn said he was 'the handsomest man on God's earth') – was there, too, and became Haydn's friend and patron. Next season Haydn often conducted the musical soirées at Carlton House. By 20 December, Haydn had already heard of Mozart's death on 5 December. 'For some time I was beside myself', he wrote to Puchberg, the Viennese banker who had made Mozart's final years financially possible. And to another friend he wrote, 'Posterity will not see such a talent as his for the next hundred years'.

Meanwhile Haydn's phenomenal success in London had not gone unnoticed by Salomon's rivals, the Professional Concerts. They accordingly got hold of Haydn's popular and fashionable pupil Ignaz Pleyel, who was at that time at Strasbourg, and engaged him as their 'composer in residence'. The Professional Concerts stirred up a war in the newspapers, but as soon as Pleyel arrived, Haydn embraced him and was the first to applaud his pupil's clever but rather superficial productions; it was obvious to the musicians that Pleyel was simply not in Haydn's class.

Haydn's first new symphony for the 1792 season was No. 93, which was played at Hanover Square on 17 February 1792. It was even more sensationally successful than had been the works of the previous season. *The Times*, which had hitherto ignored Haydn's presence in England, could no longer resist:

> A new Overture [this was the English term for symphony in those days] from the pen of the incomparable *Haydn*, formed one considerable branch of this stupendous musical tree [Salomon's programme]. Such a combination of excellence was contained in every movement, as inspired all the performers as well as the audience with enthusiastic ardour. Novelty of idea, agreeable caprice, and whim combined with all *Haydn's* sublime and wonted grandeur, gave additional consequence to the *soul* and feelings of every individual present. The Critic's eye brightened with additional lustre – then was the moment that the great Painter might have caught – that, which cannot be thrown on the human frame, but on such rare and great occasions. . . .

It must have been an incredible experience to go out the morning after such a concert and to buy the newspapers, each one of which contained such extravagant praise. In fact Haydn's life was moving at a giddy pace. He had fallen in love with the English widow of a German composer, and Rebecca Schroeter – we have her love letters to Haydn – must have been very different from the bigoted Frau Haydn or the superficial Italian mistress Luigia Polzelli with whom Haydn had attempted to while away the lonely evenings at Esterház. He was the toast of London, and hostesses vied with each other to have the modest but witty composer for dinner. 'It was the happiest time of my life,' said Haydn later.

Symphony No. 98 was first performed at the third Salomon concert, on 2 March. Haydn played a short 'Passage of attractive Brilliancy' on the harpsichord or pianoforte (we are not quite sure which instrument he used at the concerts, probably the latter), and the first and last movements were repeated. At the fourth concert on 9 March, Haydn first conducted his famous *Sinfonia concertante* – in the autograph only the second part of the double title was used – for violin, cello, oboe, bassoon, and orchestra, wherein (we read in the *Morning Herald*) 'Salomon particularly exerted himself on this occasion, in doing justice to the music of his friend Haydn'. At the sixth concert, 23 March, Symphony No. 94 was first given, and was a hit from the start. It soon became known as the *Surprise* because of the loud chord that interrupts the soft beginning of the *andante*. The final new symphony of the season was No. 97 in C.

No. 93, with its bold, fanfare-like beginning, is very much a symphony 'for the English taste'. The forthright energy and gay, sweeping tuttis of the outer movements are characteristic of the works written in England. Haydn thought the original version of the finale weak, but what these weaknesses were we shall never know, since only the final product has survived. It is in the slow movement of No. 93, a finely wrought theme and variations, that we see most clearly the benefits of critical London taste. In earlier works, those slow movements which succeeded best were quiet but intense in feeling, usually adagios such as Nos. 86/II and 92/II rather than andantes or allegrettos. In those two earlier symphonies, and especially in No. 92, the *minore* sections show that Haydn soon appreciated that a dramatic section in the minor key was necessary for contrast, particularly if the thematic material is very lyrical. This new dramatic impetus is repeated in the slow movement of the first London symphony, No. 96, and again in No. 93/II. It is also characteristic that trumpets and drums should now figure in most of the slow movements; No. 98 is the last work without them in the *adagio*. In No. 93/II, Haydn again draws on the *solo-tutti* principle, for the movement opens with the theme announced by a solo string quartet. The first section in the minor seems particularly weighty and significant, and the dotted rhythm of the theme becomes Handelian in its massiveness; Haydn had now been introduced to Handel on a large scale, and he had been quite overwhelmed ('I wept like a child' during the Hallelujah Chorus in *Messiah*, he said). There is always humour in Haydn's make-up and here it bounces to the fore in a ridiculous bassoon solo, marked *ff* and on low C, which comes after a particularly ethereal exchange between flutes and violins.

In No. 94, the *Surprise*, we see clearly the two opposing qualities that make the London symphonies so successful: virtuoso treatment of form and orchestration combined with extreme subtlety of musical language. It is very hard to write an innocent melody, such as that of No. 94/II, and to make it sound sophisticated as well as *semplice* (Haydn's own marking): the theme and its treatment show that simplicity such as this requires the hand of a genius. His London audiences understood Haydn's intention at once, for after the première, the critic of the *Morning Herald* wrote that 'the subject . . . was remarkably simple, but extended to vast complication'. The virtuoso element is stunningly revealed in the finale, a sonata rondo that races at a mad pace through key after key – scintillating, exhilarating, a relentless *moto perpetuo* whose violin writing shows graphically the fabulous technique his string section must have had.

As to the origin of the *Concertante* in B flat, there seems little doubt that Salomon persuaded Haydn to write it because of the great popularity of Pleyel's *sinfonie concertanti*. The Professional Concerts, in their third evening (27 February 1792), gave a new *Concertante* by Pleyel which was very well received by the Press ('Of . . . the Concertante it will be sufficiency of praise to say, that Haydn might own with honour these works of his Pupil'). Haydn's *Concertante* gives each of the four soloists a generous part, and its friendly, happy spirit, even in the pastoral slow movement, is untouched by deeper currents of emotion. One feature of the piece is unique for this late period. In the finale, Haydn returns to his Symphony No. 7, *Le Midi*, composed thirty-one years before, for a telling orchestral device: the use of an operatic recitative, in which the solo violin takes the place of the dramatic soprano. But where in No. 7 this is a serious piece of imagery, in the *Concertante* it is used as a comic, mock-heroic introduction to the frolicking theme of the finale.

Symphonies Nos. 97 and 98 are perhaps the finest of the first six Salomon symphonies. No. 97 is the last in the long and interesting series of trumpet symphonies in C, except that the meaning 'trumpet' has lost some of its previous significance in that Haydn now writes trumpets and drums in every symphony. No. 97 brilliantly sums up the C major type of work of which we have noticed a number in this essay. The first movement thunders out repeated Cs and Gs with a ferocious drive that we have come to associate mainly with Beethoven, and the splendid minuet, with its flaming orchestral colour and crashing timpani solo, as well as the dashing virtuosity of the finale – all these things reflect the glory of Haydn's first English sojourn. The slow movement is particularly successful, a fusion of wisdom and elegance. In it, one encounters some revealing technical instructions, such as *sul ponticello* (on the bridge of the violin), which shows that Haydn was now forced to write down things which he had previously communicated orally to his players. In the trio of the minuet, he writes over the last stanza of the violin part an indication that a solo violin should play simultaneously with the tutti violins but an octave higher: he marks this 'Salomon Solo ma piano' (Salomon alone but quietly). And this remark exemplifies the character of the Salomon symphonies: inspiration encouraged by favourable conditions.

In Symphony No. 98, Haydn used trumpets and kettledrums in the key of B flat, as he did in the *Concertante* noticed above: so far as we can tell, this is the first time in the history of the symphony, and possibly altogether, that a composer used trumpets and timpani in that key. (Mozart never did, for instance.) Perhaps it was an English speciality or perhaps Haydn himself invented the idea; he exported it to Vienna later, writing many of the choral movements in the *Creation* and *Seasons*, and four of the last six Masses, in B flat with trumpets and drums. It is also typical of Haydn that he should invent a modern notation for the kettle-drums in that key: instead of writing them in C-G, *i.e.* as transposing instruments (which is what Mozart and many other composers did), Haydn writes them at correct pitch, with (in the case of B flat) one flat in the signature: the other flat sign – for E flat – was superfluous in that the timpani only played in B flat and F. We mention this rather technical matter only to show that Haydn was always ahead of the times, and that he was a musician's musician, always thinking of things to make the player's life easier. The idea of writing something that the players could not play or the singers not sing without enormous difficulty, as Beethoven was to do, would have seemed lunacy to Haydn, and indeed to Mozart. In the London of 1792, the composer, players, audience, and critics were closer than they were ever to be again, and so we have the curious paradox that while Haydn's music was forward-looking and 'modern', it was the last time, almost, that there was no mental gap between the intelligent listener and the composer. That gap has now widened almost to the point of no return; it has taken forty years for *Wozzeck* to become part of the operatic repertoire and thirty years before Covent Garden staged *Moses and Aaron*.

Not only 'Salomon Solo' appears in No. 98: as we have noted above there is also 'Haydn Solo' (not *ma piano* . . .) in the finale. Although this is a sonata movement, Haydn never displayed to better advantage his grasp of the variation technique, for the theme constantly recurs. Towards the end it appears in a coda, marked *più moderato* (more moderately), but the strings can now play semiquavers and it soon appears that this section is in fact faster than the preceding music. Once again the theme returns, and over it Haydn wrote for himself in the autograph a series of broken arpeggios on the pianoforte which provide a silvery background for the end of this radiant movement. Small wonder that the cheering audience that March night at the Hanover Square Rooms demanded that it should be repeated.

The first movement of No. 98 begins with an *adagio* which contains, in the tonic minor and at half the speed, the principal theme of the *allegro*. The movement is more sombre than others of the first London series, and the development bursts into a magnificent and wholly serious contrapuntal extension of the first subject, which grows increasingly turbulent and chromatic as it delves into remoter tonal regions. Sir Donald Tovey thought the second movement, based on a melody obviously inspired by 'God save the King', was Haydn's lament for the death of Mozart, and indeed the tragic overtones of late Mozart are never far away in this wonderful and searching music. No. 98 is spiritually the link to the second set of Salomon symphonies: more than any of its fellows, it contains that carefully measured combination of light and dark, that mixture of various emotions which masterpieces in the arts generally have.

On 12 April 1792, the *Public Advertiser* printed the following note: 'Haydn finds the *good cheer* of this country in such *concert pitch* with his own *great taste*, that he has declared his intention of concluding the *finale* of his days, with the "Roast Beef of Old England".' There is no doubt that Haydn was seriously contemplating a transference of his allegiance from Austria to England. He received a generous pension from the late Prince Nicolaus Esterházy, and Prince Anton did not require his services; to leave his wife was obviously more pleasure than pain; and he had made, in the two years he had stayed in England, 12,000 *Gulden*, or the equivalent of twelve years' salary at Esterház. There was in fact every inducement for him to settle permanently in a country that loved and respected him, and was willing to make him, if anything, richer and more famous. It was obviously Haydn's intention to return to Vienna, settle his affairs, and move to London for good.

Haydn did return to England again, but he did not stay permanently, although the King and Queen offered him lodgings in Windsor Castle. Possibly the war with France had something to do with Haydn's decision to return to Austria; possibly he felt that he was not up to a life of such constant tensions and pressures – after all, he was in his sixties; and possibly the death of Prince Anton, a few days after Haydn left Vienna in January 1794, and the succession to the title of Prince Nicolaus II, who wanted to reconstitute the band and have Haydn to direct it, proved a decisive factor.

For the second English visit, Haydn took his valet and copyist Johann Elssler, who wrote out all the orchestral parts in his clear, flowing hand (Haydn had found 'a dearth of good copyists' in England on the previous visit). When he arrived in London, he carried with him the finished score of No. 99 and sections of Nos. 100 and 101. No. 99 was played for the first time on 10 February, a mere five days after Haydn's arrival. The orchestra this time was larger and included clarinets, which are used for the first time in a Haydn symphony in No. 99. (All the others except No. 102 now have these instruments.) The next work was No. 101 (the *Clock*) – of the last six symphonies, the chronology is correct except that the positions of Nos. 100 and 101 should be reversed – which Haydn conducted on 3 March. The *Oracle* noted, of No. 101, that 'the connoisseurs admit [it] to be his best work'. The third work was No. 100 (the *Military*), given at Hanover Square on 31 March 1794, and it was the greatest success of Haydn's whole life.

> Another new Symphony [wrote the *Morning Chronicle* after the second performance] by Haydn, was performed for the second time; and the middle movement was again received with absolute shouts of applause. Encore! encore! encore! resounded from every seat: the Ladies themselves could not forbear. . . .

The difficulty of persuading singers from the Continent to make guest appearances in London forced Salomon, in January 1795, to cancel his series; but in their stead came the Opera Concerts, with a very large orchestra of sixty players, under the leadership of the famous Italian violinist G. B. Viotti. Salomon was involved with the concerts, of course, and also appeared as a soloist. It was for these Opera Concerts that Haydn wrote his last three symphonies, Nos. 102, 103 (*Drum Roll*) and 104 (*London*), the first in the summer and autumn of 1794 and the others in 1795. No. 102 was first given on 2 February ('What shall we say of Haydn, and the sublime, the magic Overture [Symphony], with which he began the second part? The rapture it gave cannot be communicated by words: to be known it must be heard.' *Morning Chronicle*), No. 103 on 2 March ('The Introduction excited the deepest attention. . . .' *Morning Chronicle*), and No. 104 probably on 13 April 1795.

At Haydn's benefit concert on 4 May, he conducted, apart from works by other composers, the *Military* and *London* Symphonies, a duet from his earlier opera *Orlando Paladino*, and possibly his greatest operatic work, the *Scena di Berenice*, which he wrote for the occasion. His diary notes: 'The whole company was very pleased and so was I. I made 4,000 *Gulden* [then £400, now about £3,000] on this evening: such a thing is possible only in England.'

The second set of Salomon symphonies is divided, both chronologically and musically, into two groups: those performed at the Salomon Concerts in 1794 (Nos. 99–101), and those for the Opera Concerts of 1795 (Nos. 102–104).

If the second movement of No. 98 is regarded as Haydn's tribute to Mozart, the *adagio* of No. 99, written in Vienna in 1793, is even more of a personal farewell: Haydn's beloved friend Marianna von Genzinger had died, apparently of cancer, at the beginning of the year, and it requires no biographer to tell us of the loneliness, the emptiness that Haydn must have felt at the loss. He tells us what she meant to him in this wonderful, heart-searching movement, and in the coda to the *Andante con variazioni* in F minor, perhaps Haydn's finest piano piece. Among the many beauties of this lyrical and emotionally charged symphonic movement, I would call attention to the extraordinary windband passage, towards the beginning, which so struck the London critics; and to the fact that Haydn saves his trumpets and timpani for the middle of the section after the double bar, where they enter in C major. (A word about the tonality: the symphony is in E flat, the second movement in G, the so-called mediant; C is the submediant.) The trio is also written in C, and in order to get back to E flat, the home key, Haydn writes a lead-back from the end of the trio to the *da capo* of the minuet, something he was also to do in No. 104.

The *Military* Symphony reminds us that Haydn was writing for the most glittering and sophisticated audience in Europe at that time; *fin de siècle* London must have equalled in brilliance that of the *ancien régime* in Pre-Revolutionary Paris, and in London it was a free and highly civilized society that paid its homage to Haydn. Some of the glitter appears in this symphony: for instance in the coda of the first movement, which is pure joy in the sound of a large orchestra, beautifully disciplined, but which further investigation reveals as a still further thematic development of the second subject. The slow movement is adapted from that of an earlier (1786) Concerto for the King of Naples, where it was scored for two *lire organizzate*, horns, and strings with divided violas. (Haydn retained the divided violas but of course re-orchestrated the movement.) The rather theatrical coda, with its trumpet call and the thunderous timpani solo are the outward trappings with which Haydn encouraged his London audience to respond with 'shouts of joy', and there is an equally dramatic timpani entrance in the finale. But Haydn always wrote for the connoisseurs as well as the crowd, and there are fascinating things in every movement for the musician. The wind instruments are used with great boldness and originality throughout the second set, and though this tendency is clearly seen in the famous windband passage in the development of No. 97/I, almost every one of the last six works has striking solo passages for the woodwind and indeed for

brass and timpani. The first subject of No. 100/I – after the slow introduction – is scored for flutes and oboes only, and looks forward to the
'toy' music of Rimsky-Korsakov.

No. 101 has always been a popular work, and rightly so. The finale
has claims to being the greatest final movement Haydn ever wrote, a
breathtaking sonata rondo with everything in it from a virtuoso double
fugue (all held down to *pianissimo*) to D minor interludes of Beethoven-
ian power and panache. The symphony's fame, however, comes from the
witty slow movement, where the accompaniments move in measured,
'clock'-like quavers: here, too, a gigantic section in the minor jolts us
out of the ticking sophistication of the earlier parts, and the clock
quavers are battered out by horns and trumpets.

Nos. 102–104, especially the first and last of the trio, while inspired
and encouraged by the continuing success of the second English journey,
rise far above the circumstances in which they were produced. These three
works, with their strange harmonic tendencies and depth of expression,
look many decades into the future. Haydn was obviously quite aware of
their significance, and it is no accident that his personal 'In Nomine
Domini' appears twice in No. 102, not only at the beginning but also at
the beginning of the extraordinary slow movement. The title page of No.
104 reads, 'The 12th I have composed in England'. With these three
symphonies, Haydn reached the pinnacle of his symphonic art.

No. 102 shows one direction that young composers could have followed: it is an essay in compactness, in expressing a powerful thought in
the shortest possible form. It is certainly one of Haydn's loudest and
most aggressive works so far as its outer movements are concerned, and
both the slow introduction and the *adagio* are among the greatest things
of their kind. The first movement is a fantastic and brilliant essay in
sonata form, with a positively thrilling development section, in which a
fragment of one theme serves to build a canon which stamps up and
down the orchestra, its already terrific force doubled by the use of *forzati*:
a hair-raising timpani roll shoots the music into the recapitulation,
which appears, after the tumult of the development section, like a dazz-
ling conqueror. The *adagio* is a curious and immensely powerful
movement, where one always senses – and once or twice feels – the
rippling muscles underneath the smoothly flowing surface. Haydn uses
muted trumpets and covered kettledrums, and a solo cello, which gives
a slightly sinister undertone (in the case of the first two instruments) to
the whole. The movement was apparently a favourite of Rebecca Schroeter, Haydn's English woman friend, and he used it as the middle

movement of the F sharp minor Piano Trio, dedicated to her. The finale is a dashing sonata rondo with a sense of humour; Haydn's wit was something the English adored, and it is characteristic that this was the movement they made him repeat when the work was first performed.

If No. 102 is an exercise in dramatic brevity, No. 103 is one of the longest of all Haydn's symphonies. The first movement is unusual and daring: the opening, a solo drum roll, is unique in symphonic litera-ture. The rather ominous slow introduction forms the later course of the movement in several ways. For one thing it is introduced, speeded up, in the development section; then, after an almost doom-ridden series of *ff decresc.*, the fast section stops and the drum roll and slow introduction return, to be broken off for the conclusion, again in fast tempo. On paper this may sound prosaic, but its effect on a late-eighteenth-century audience must have been stupendous. Because of this innovation, the symphony is known as the *Drum Roll*. The slow movement is a double variation, of which both sections are based on Eastern European folk-tunes (notice the typically 'Slavonic' progression of the opening, G-C-D-E flat-F sharp-G); the first is in the minor, the second in the major. Haydn lingers over the music, the folk-tune originals of which he obviously loved; when it seems that the movement will end, he modulates and brings in a large coda.

All his life Haydn experimented with monothematicism: that is, with the possibility of dropping the second subject altogether or, at any rate, rendering it structurally of secondary importance. In No. 103/IV he constructs the whole movement on one theme, and thereby sets himself a particularly hard task; needless to say he brings it off with dash and vigour, and it is an astonishing tribute to his ingenuity that although there is only one theme, it is varied so deftly that one is hardly conscious of the all-present monothematicism. By way of introducing the theme, he has a short fanfare for the horns, a series of chords which also prove to be the accompaniment of the principal subject. In essence, Haydn has now created a form where all the individual parts, however secondary they may at first appear, have a vital structural task to fulfil.

One might almost say that Haydn's last symphony, No. 104 in D, became part of the standard repertoire the day after the first perform-ance. It is a work as typical of Haydn as, say, *Eine kleine Nachtmusik* is typical of Mozart; the 'London' Symphony seems to sum up, in one vast canvas, Haydn's symphonic style. We have the slow introduction, a portentous D minor opening with a dotted unison figure that empha-sizes the two most important notes of D minor (or major) – the tonic and the fifth (A). The whole introduction is in a tiny three-part form, with miniature exposition, development, and recapitulation. After such a dramatic opening, the principal subject of Haydn's *allegro* is a classic example of a singing theme. When he gets to the dominant, the theme enters again, so that the proper second subject has the quality of a little epilogue. Even in the exposition, Haydn modulates, and uses for his tuttis sections of the main theme. For the development he uses six notes from the first subject and establishes a most dramatic atmosphere, after which the lyrical main theme *in toto* comes like a release.

The second movement, too, is a kind of summing-up: there is the (by now regular) explosion in the minor, when trumpets and timpani enter for the first time; there is a wistful series of pauses (fermatas) with solo flute, and above all a kind of coda where the music pours forth in a quiet stream of emotion, as if Haydn knew (as he no doubt did) that this was to be his last symphonic slow movement. In the minuet there are off-beat accents which give an Eastern European tinge to the robust melody, and in the second section there is a famous timpani *crescendo* to lead in the recapitulation. The trio is in B flat, which is reached by what is known as a pivot note: in this case D, which is both the tonic of the old and the third of the new key. As in No. 99/III, there is an extended lead-back to the *da capo* of the minuet.

The finale is supposed to be based on an English street-cry ('hot cross buns'), but whatever country the theme comes from – one of Smetana's *Czech Dances* for piano is based on a variant and the Croats say it is a melody of theirs – it has a strong folk-song quality. Combining art with science, Haydn has worked out the second subject so that it can be combined with the first – which he does immediately after the double bar, at the beginning of the development section. In this classic finale, too, Haydn lingers over his music more than usual: there are episodes where time almost seems to stop, and when Haydn's farewell to the symphony must have been heart-wrenching. But the music's the thing, and Haydn finishes off his last symphony with a rousing tutti, to conclude nearly forty years of constant and loving labour with a form that he had done so much to perfect.

In its issue of 21 November 1798, the Leipzig *Allgemeine musikalische Zeitung* carried a biographical note about Mozart, in which he is quoted as saying: 'But there is no one who can do it all – to joke and to terrify, to evoke laughter and profound sentiment – and all equally well: except Joseph Haydn.' It could stand as a motto to Haydn's hundred symphonies.

Index of Symphonies

Bold figures refer to main entries